The Poets and the Fathers

The Poets and the Fathers

Theology and Poetry
from Gregory Nazianzus to Scott Cairns

TIMOTHY E. G. BARTEL

☙PICKWICK *Publications* • Eugene, Oregon

THE POETS AND THE FATHERS
Theology and Poetry from Gregory Nazianzus to Scott Cairns

Copyright © 2024 Timothy E. G. Bartel. All rights reserved. Except for brief quotations in critical publications or reviews, no part of this book may be reproduced in any manner without prior written permission from the publisher. Write: Permissions, Wipf and Stock Publishers, 199 W. 8th Ave., Suite 3, Eugene, OR 97401.

Pickwick Publications
An Imprint of Wipf and Stock Publishers
199 W. 8th Ave., Suite 3
Eugene, OR 97401

www.wipfandstock.com

PAPERBACK ISBN: 978-1-6667-8790-0
HARDCOVER ISBN: 978-1-6667-8791-7
EBOOK ISBN: 978-1-6667-8792-4

Cataloguing-in-Publication data:

Names: Bartel, Timothy E. G. [author]

Title: The poets and the fathers : theology and poetry from Gregory Nazianzus to Scott Cairns / Timothy E. G. Bartel.

Description: Eugene, OR: Pickwick Publications, 2024 | Includes bibliographical references.

Identifiers: ISBN 978-1-6667-8790-0 (paperback) | ISBN 978-1-6667-8791-7 (hardcover) | ISBN 978-1-6667-8792-4 (ebook)

Subjects: LCSH: Christian poetry, Early—History and criticism. | Christian poetry, English—History and criticism. | Fathers of the Church. | Christianity and literature. | Poetry.

Classification: PN1077 B37 2024 (print) | PN1077 (ebook)

Contents

Acknowledgments vii

1. Introduction: The Poets and the Fathers 1
2. Gregory Nazianzus and the Poetry of Orthodox Life 16
3. The Sweetened List: The Strange Case of Gregory Nazianzus's Poem on the Biblical Canon 41
4. A New Macrina: Toward a Cappadocian Poetics for the Twenty-First Century 51
5. The Virtue of Silence: Ethics and Quietude in the Poems of Henry Wadsworth Longfellow 67
6. From "The Soul" to "The Warning": Longfellow, Education, and Abolition 77
7. Prudentius among the Moderns: The *Cathemerinon* Hymns in the Work of C. S. Lewis and T. S. Eliot 91
8. Scott Cairns as Syriac Poet: Reading the Eastern in *Idiot Psalms* 104
9. Conclusion: The Literary Conservationist 110

Bibliography 115

Acknowledgments

Many of the following essays, in earlier forms, were first presented as conference papers or retreat speeches, including the following:

"The Poets and the Fathers" was first presented at the Saint Constantine Vision Conference, summer 2022.

"Gregory Nazianzus and the Poetry of Orthodox Life" was first presented at the Saint George Orthodox Church Lenten Retreat, spring 2023.

"The Sweetened List" was first presented at the Houston Baptist University Theology Conference, spring 2017.

"A New Macrina" was first presented at the Emerging Scholars Colloquium at Duke University, summer 2019.

"The Virtue of Silence" was first presented at the Southwest Conference for Christianity and Literature at Houston Baptist University, fall 2013.

"From 'The Soul' to 'The Warning'" was first presented at the American Literature Association's Symposium on American Poetry in Washington, DC, winter 2020.

Acknowledgments

"Prudentius among the Moderns" was first presented at the Southwest Conference for Christianity and Literature at Abilene Christian University—Dallas Campus, fall 2017.

"The Literary Conservationist" was first presented at the Circe National Conference in Austin, TX, summer 2017.

Permissions:

Slow Pilgrim by Scott Cairns
Copyright 2015 by Scott Cairns
Used by permission of Paraclete Press

The Poems of Prudentius, Volume 1 by Prudentius
Copyright 1962 by The Catholic University of America Press, Inc.
Used with kind permission of Catholic University of America Press

1

Introduction

The Poets and the Fathers

> The eloquence of the Christian Fathers flowed from a purer fountain than the streams of classic poetry . . . bright with the glories of revelation and radiant with a more than earthly splendor.[1]

WE MIGHT EXPECT THE above words to appear in a sermon by a pastor or bishop, someone keen to defend the writings of the Christian past against any comparison to the "classic" pagan writings of antiquity. But curiously, these words appear in a nineteenth-century lecture presented in the Harvard modern languages department, and they were written by the Unitarian poet Henry Wadsworth Longfellow. Longfellow was a deep lover of classical literature; he was a keen reader of Homer and Virgil and he published translations from Ovid. But throughout his professional life, he esteemed one group of writers as more important than the pagan classics for not only Christians, but for all lovers of literature: the Church Fathers.

It is my contention that Longfellow is instructive in two important ways. First, his literal claim is correct: the eloquence and

---

1. Wagenknecht, *Longfellow*, 290.

glories of the writings of the Church Fathers do arguably surpass those of the pagans, especially inasmuch as they reveal and contemplate the Triune God who reveals Himself in scripture. But second, Longfellow's words are instructive because they suggest that the conventional approach to the study of English literature, and poetry in particular, may be misguided. We must reject an approach to English poetry that sees religious traditions in general—and early Christian thought in particular—as either irrelevant or hostile to literary endeavor and innovation. In opposition to this, I wish to show how the Church Fathers are embedded in the thought and tradition of English poetry. Early in my own career as a scholar, Longfellow's words suggested to me something that started as a hunch and has become a conviction: that English literature is not entirely understandable without reference to and a knowledge of the Church Fathers.

Let me share with you a worry I have about literary education, especially that literary education which is informed by the tradition of classical education. It is commonplace in such contexts to begin a course of study with Homer and read the classics chronologically up through the modern age: Homer, Virgil, Dante, Shakespeare, Milton, Austen. This list alone is worth years of study. But this list is also illustrative of a defect in our approach to the classics. Let's take a look at the time periods it covers: Homer wrote around the seventh century BC, Virgil wrote in the first century BC, Dante wrote in the fourteenth century AD, Shakespeare in the sixteenth century, Milton in the seventeenth, Austen in the nineteenth. There is an obvious 1,200-year gap between Virgil and Dante.

What do we usually read in between them? If we are keen on English literature, we will probably read *Beowulf*; and if we are interested in theology, we will likely read some key Church Fathers, most often Augustine, but sometimes also Justin Martyr, Athanasius, and Boethius. We can trace the development of Latin theology, especially, from Augustine through Boethius to Thomas Aquinas, and then see the employment of a millennium of Latin theology in Dante's *Commedia*. Literature, it can seem to us, takes

INTRODUCTION

a little break for 800 years, from Virgil until *Beowulf*, and then really gets going again with Dante, Chaucer, and Shakespeare. Historically, of course, this notion is just plain false. I would like to map out for you a brief history of early Christian literature so that we may better understand how the English poetic tradition and the Church Fathers are connected.

First, it must be understood that Christian poetry is as old as Christian prose. At the same time that the Apostolic Fathers like Saint Ignatius of Antioch and Saint Clement of Rome were writing their epistles to the churches, Christian poetry began to appear. The most important of these early poems were the *Odes of Solomon*, hymns of praise to Christ written by an anonymous, likely Syrian writer in the early second century AD. By the end of the second century, hymns and homilies in Greek verse had begun to appear, written by prominent bishops like Clement of Alexandria and Melito of Sardis. The third century boasted literary artists like Methodius, who wrote a poetic dialogue about Saint Thecla. At this time anonymous Greek hymns like the *Phos Ilarion* also began to be incorporated into liturgical practice.

It was in the fourth century especially that patristic poetry blossomed and came into its own. Early in the century the Christian scholar Lactantius composed an allegorical poem on the phoenix as a Christ-allegory, followed shortly by Juvencus, who was the first to write the gospel story in the form of a Latin epic poem with Christ as its hero. Around this time Saint Hilary of Poitiers began to experiment with original hymns in Latin verse, inspired in part by spending time in Christian Syria. In Syria, a remarkable hymnic tradition had emerged through the writings of Ephrem, the great genius of Nisibis. Not to be outdone by the Syrians and Latins, Greek Christian poetry began to flourish in the second half of the fourth century, especially in the writings of Gregory Nazianzus, but also in the hymns of Synesius of Cyrene. A new generation of Latin poets built upon the earlier work of Juvencus, Lactantius, and Hilary, and brought the Latin Christian epic, hymn, and allegory into more complex and mature forms. Chief among these late fourth-century Latin writers were Ambrose, Proba, Paulinus, and

Prudentius. Gregory Nazianzus and Prudentius are particularly of note for the number of genres in which they excelled. Gregory wrote hymns, autobiography, epigrams, sermons, and possibly even a tragedy in classical Greek verse; Prudentius wrote hymns, epigrams, apologetic diatribes, scriptural commentaries, and wild, violent allegories, all in polished Latin poetry. And this is to say nothing of the foundational writing in prose that many of these writers composed. Ephrem, Gregory, and Ambrose were especially important to the development of the Christian sermon and Trinitarian theology in the fourth century. These were no mere pious artisans who established the early Christian literary tradition. They were bishops, evangelists, apologists, and theologians, and their poetry was part of their wholistic Christian witness to the ages.

This is all well and good, you may say, but we are still a long way from John Milton and T. S. Eliot! Patience, I answer. The fourth-century literary renaissance established the major genres of the Christian literary tradition that would continue for the next few centuries: Juvencus and Proba began the biblical epic tradition that would continue with Nonnus and Sedulius in the fifth century and Arator in the sixth century. Ephrem, Ambrose, and Prudentius established a hymnic tradition that would be developed by Sedulius and Jacob of Serug in the fifth century, Romanos and Columba in the sixth century, and John of Damascus and Caedmon in the seventh century.

And with the names Columba and Caedmon I have tipped my hat to my argument. For Saint Columba of Iona and Caedmon are both Christian writers at the dawn of the English poetic tradition. Columba was an Anglo-Latin bishop and Caedmon was the very first composer of a Christian hymn in Anglo-Saxon. It is in Caedmon that we first meet the term *middle-earth* (*middengeard*) in English poetry. Columba, Caedmon, and the other major English writers of the late first millennium—Alcman, Bede, Alfred, and the Beowulf poet—wrote in an Orthodox Christian context and took the writings of the Church Fathers, both prose and poetry, as their models and precursors. Thus we have, emerging around the same time as *Beowulf*, biblical epics in Anglo-Saxon which retell narratives from Genesis and Exodus, taking as models the work of writers like Juvencus and Proba. In fact, both *Beowulf* and the Anglo-Saxon Exodus epic begin in the same way: "*Hwaet,*"—or, in a more modern sense, "Listen up! A hero is about to step forth into the story."

Now, those familiar with medieval and Renaissance history may be wondering whether this continuity between early English literature and early Christian literature is simply a feature of the early Middle Ages. In many accounts of the Renaissance and Enlightenment, we find that the writers of these eras are characterized by a rejection of Christian late antiquity and the Middle Ages. We may especially expect to find this in English Protestant poetry. Let us look next to Milton—that most Puritan of English poets—and see what we find.

MILTON AND EARLY CHRISTIAN POETRY

Whole books have been written on Milton's theological sources, which range from the ante-Nicene Church Fathers through the theologians of the English reformation, but less has been said about the influence of the Church Fathers' poetry on Milton's verse. We know from the commonplace book kept by Milton in the 1630s and '40s that he read works by Clement, Lactantius, and Prudentius, and was likely familiar with at least Clement's "Hymn to Christ" from the *Pedagogue*, Prudentius's hagiographic hymns in the *Libra Peristephanon*, and Lactatius's phoenix poem.[2] The image of the phoenix in particular plays an important role in Milton's 1645 Latin poem "Epitaphium Damonis." In the second to last stanza of the poem, the shepherd Thyrsis laments the death of his friend Damon, saying that he will never get to show Damon a beautiful cup, on which there is a picture of a phoenix. In Latin, Milton's line about the phoenix runs: "Has inter Phoenix, divina

---

2. Milton, *Common-Place Book*, 1, 8, 13, 38.

avis, unica terris."[3] In literal English this reads: "Within these [trees] the phoenix, divine bird, unique on earth." This line is similar to the line in which Lactantius introduces the phoenix: "hos nemus, hos lucos avis incolit unica phoenix."[4] In literal English, Lactantius's line reads: "In this grove, in this wood, a bird lives, the unique phoenix." Milton both imitates the placement of the phoenix within a wooded area and borrows Lactantius's word "unica" to describe the singular nature of the phoenix.

Milton uses the phoenix image to further his tragic scene of the inability of the living to share an experience of beauty with the dead. In doing this, Milton downplays the primarily allegorical significance of the phoenix that is found in Lactantius. However, Milton reminds us of the theological nature of the source-poem through his usage of the adjective "divina." Further, the reader of Milton who also knows Lactantius will remember that these early Christian writers explicitly used the phoenix as an image of the resurrection for which all Christians hope, and thus the presence of the phoenix image in the "Epitaphium Damonis" retains a reminder of the hope of resurrection even in the midst of tragic grief.

Speaking of tragedy, one of the major places in Milton's poetry that early Christian poetry is explicitly mentioned is in the prefatory essay to his 1671 verse tragedy *Samson Agonistes*. This essay, titled "Of that Sort of Dramatic Poem which is Called Tragedy," begins with Milton's defense of his choice to write a tragedy:

> Tragedy, as it was anciently composed, hath been ever held the gravest, moralest, and most profitable of all other poems: therefore said by Aristotle to be of power by raising pity and fear, or terror, to purge the mind of those and such like passions, that is to temper and reduce them to just measure with a kind of delight, stirred up by reading or seeing those passions well imitated. ... Gregory Nazianzen a Father of the Church, thought it not unbeseeming the sanctity of his person to write a Tragedy, which he entitled, Christ Suffering. This is mentioned to vindicate Tragedy from the small esteem,

---

3. Milton, *Major Works*, 158.
4. Lactantius, "Phoenix," 28.

Introduction

or rather infamy, which in the account of many it undergoes at this day with other common interludes; happening through the poet's error of intermixing Comic stuff with Tragic sadness and gravity; or introducing trivial and vulgar persons, which by all judicious hath been counted absurd; and brought in without discretion, corruptly to gratify the people.[5]

Milton seems concerned that his contemporaries are averse to the very idea of tragedies. He chalks this up not to the tragic genre itself, but to the misguided "intermixing" of comedy and tragedy. Milton reminds his readers that, according to Aristotle, tragedy is the most exalted form of poetry, and he gives as an example of worthy tragedy the *Christos Paschon* of Saint Gregory Nazianzus. Though the *Christos Paschon* is not mentioned in Milton's commonplace book alongside the other Church Fathers mentioned above, it is unsurprising that Milton would have been familiar with it, for it was a poem of some interest to the literary world of sixteenth and seventeenth-century Europe. This can especially be seen in the works of Hugo Grotius, who wrote a 1608 Latin play in imitation of Gregory's tragedy, which he titled *Christus Patiens*.

The conclusion of *Samson Agonistes* involves the chorus's grave celebration of Samson's destruction of the Philistines, and in the midst of these lines, the chorus uses a familiar figure to describe Samson:

> So virtue given for lost,
> Deprest, and overthrown, as seemed,
> Like that self-begotten bird
> In the Arabian woods embost,
> That no second knows nor third,
> And lay erewhile a holocaust,
> From out her ashy womb now teemed
> Revives, reflourishes, then vigorous most
> When most unactive deemed,
> And though her body die, her fame survives,
> A secular bird ages of lives.[6]

5. Milton, *Major Works*, 671.
6. Milton, *Major Works*, 714.

The chorus here compares Samson's final defiance of the Philistines to our old friend the phoenix. The phoenix here is no longer described as "unicam," nor "divina,"—indeed now Milton calls it not a "divine bird," but, curiously, a "secular bird." This new Samsonic phoenix is "self-begotten," another quality found in and explored at length in Lactantius's poem. In the final two lines of the speech, Milton provides a twist on the resurrection theme associated with the phoenix. Though Samson's body has perished in his overthrow of the Philistines, his "fame" will survive for many "ages of lives."

It would seem perverse to end our discussion of Milton and the early Christian poets without mentioning Milton's biblical epics *Paradise Lost* and *Paradise Regained*. But of these poems in relation to early Christian poetry, it is difficult to speak with much confidence. For his biblical tragedy, Milton explicitly names Gregory Nazianzus as his patristic precursor. But Milton does not name an equivalent patristic precursor for his epics. Juvencus, Proba, and Prudentius are the obvious options, but of the three Milton names only Prudentius as among his reading, and even then, it is Prudentius's hymns, not his martial epic *Psychomachia*, that Milton clearly read. Perhaps only this can be said with surety: that if it were not for Juvencus, Proba, and Prudentius inventing it, there would be no Christian epic tradition; even if Milton did not read their epics, he is still indebted to them for inventing the genre. And, if we want to be bold, we might say that they ought to be proud of Milton, for he wrote, in *Paradise Lost*, perhaps the most masterful biblical epic of all time.

BROWNING AND EARLY CHRISTIAN POETRY

In February 1842, the London Magazine *Aetheneum* began publishing a series of articles by a young poet named Elizabeth Barrett (known to us now under her married name of Elizabeth Barrett Browning). These articles were titled "Some Account of the Greek Christian Poets" and argued for the ongoing importance and relevance of the Greek poets of the early Church. Browning begins her essays with a praise of the Greek language itself:

INTRODUCTION

> Blind Homer spoke this Greek after blind Demodocus, with a quenchless light about his brows, which he felt through his blindness. Pindar rolled his chariots in it, prolonging the clamor of the games. Sappho's heart beat through it, and heaved up the world's. Aeschylus strained it to the stature of his high thoughts. Plato crowned it with his divine peradventures. Aristophanes made it drunk with the wine of his fantastic merriment. The later Platonists wove their souls away in it, out of sight of other souls. The first Christians heard in it God's new revelation, and confessed their Christ in it from the suppliant's knee, and presently from the bishop's throne. To all times, and their transitions, the language lent itself. Reckon names "for remembrance;" and speak of things not ignoble—of meek, heroic Christians, and heavenward faces washed serene by tears—strong knees bending humbly for the very strength's sake—bright intellects burning often to the winds in fantastic shapes, but oftener still with an honest, inward heat, vehement on heart and brain. . . . Surely not ignoble things! And the reader will perceive at once that the writer's heart is not laid beneath the wheels of a cumbrous ecclesiastical antiquity, that its intent is to love what is lovable, to honor what is honorable, and to kiss both through the dust of centuries.[7]

For Browning, the early Christians are to be considered the inheritors of the Greek poetic tradition of Homer, Sappho, and Aeschylus. Browning admits that the early Christian poets are not to be considered quite the equals of these classical poets, but she urges that she writes of them in order to "reckon names 'for remembrance.'" It may be tempting to accuse Browning of damning the early Christian poets with faint praise, but throughout her "Account" she spends a generous amount of time introducing and exploring the poetry of each major Greek Christian poet.

Browning actually begins before the Christian era with Ezekiel the Tragedian and his tragedy on the book of Exodus. She then moves onto Clement of Alexandria and Gregory Nazianzus.

---

7. Browning, *Essays*, 12–13.

Though Browning is skeptical of the poetic quality of Clement's "Hymn to Christ," she is rather taken with Gregory Nazianzus, to whom she "offer[s] our earliest homage."[8] Browning had studied Greek literature with the scholar Hugh Boyd, who we may credit with instilling in Browning a high esteem of Gregory's poetry. Browning gives a sympathetic overview of Gregory's life and the character of his work, wherein she focuses on Gregory's ability to write of grief and suffering with special felicity. Browning quotes generously from her translation of several of Gregory's poems, including one she calls "rather a cry than a song":[9]

> Where are my winged words? Dissolved in air.
> Where is my flower of youth? All withered. Where
> My glory? Vanished. Where the strength I knew
> From comely limbs? Disease hath changed it too.
> And bent them. Where the riches and the lands?
> God hath THEM! Yea, and sinners' snatching hands
> I have grudged the rest. Where is my father, mother,
> And where my blessed sister, my sweet brother?
> Gone to the grave!—There did remain for me
> Alone my fatherland, till destiny,
> Malignly stirring a black tempest, drove
> My foot from that last rest. And now I rove
> Estranged and desolate a foreign shore.[10]

Though Browning explores Gregory's poetry at more length than Milton did, she is unmoved by the very work of Gregory—*Christos Paschon*—that proved most influential to the work of Milton. She is so disturbed by the work, in fact, that she ascribes its composition to the heretic Apollinarius. However frustrated this might make the reader with Browning (who, we must remember, was a world-class poet whose critical sensibilities should not be too casually dismissed), it ought to also make the reader more impressed with Gregory, whose poems are diverse enough to inspire and influence different ages and different poets in widely contrasting ways. If the

---

8. Browning, *Essays*, 29.
9. Browning, *Essays*, 39.
10. Browning, *Essays*, 39–40.

INTRODUCTION

tragic Gregory of *Christos Paschon* was the Gregory that Milton most loved, then the lyric and autobiographical Gregory of the shorter poems is the one that Browning loved most.

After her discussion of Gregory, Browning goes on to introduce and provide translations from many later Greek poets, including Synesius (who she ranks very highly) and Saint John of Damascus. Saint John's verse overall does not impress Browning like that of Gregory and Synesius, but she includes a translation of one of his hymns in which, she says, "the tears trickle audibly."[11]

With Milton we explored how the poet's reading of Church Fathers like Lactantius and Gregory Nazianzus informed his own original poetry. With Browning, we find that her first major interaction with the early Christian poets is as a translator and critic. And though she may disparage the verse of Clement and the *Christos Paschon*, her translations of their poems contain a beauty that matches her translations of her favored poets, the lyrical Gregory and Synesius. In praising these poets, and the "tears" of John of Damascus, Browning is also suggesting the genre in which the Church Fathers should most be remembered: short, personal lyric, and not didactic verse or tragedy. For her, the Christian poets are the inheritors and preservers of the tradition that the pagan poets began. Though there is a disagreement between the poets about genre, Milton and Browning agree on this: there is a continuity between the classical, the patristic, and the poetry that they themselves were writing.

LONGFELLOW AND EARLY CHRISTIAN POETRY

Browning's contemporary Henry Wadsworth Longfellow never published a book on early Christian poetry, but he did write lectures on the early Church Fathers, and mentions the poetry of the early Christians in the notes to his plays and in his fiction. In Longfellow's 1849 novella *Kavanagh* the narrator describes the protagonist as a lively and progressive young preacher, who prefers

---

11. Browning, *Essays*, 81.

the "mystic hymns of . . . Synesius" to the "odes of Pindar and Horace."¹² In another patristic reference, the narrator of *Kavanagh* laments that the protagonist no longer lived in a time when anyone would praise his sermons by crying out: "'Orthodox Chrysostom! Thirteenth Apostle! Worthy the priesthood!' as was done in the days of the Christian Fathers."¹³

In 1850 Longfellow published *The Golden Legend*, a play set in medieval Germany, which interacts with the early Christian poets in two ways. First, the main characters watch a nativity play, and in his note on this scene Longfellow provides a brief overview of the history of Christian theater:

> A singular chapter in the history of the Middle Ages is that which gives account of the early Christian Drama, the Mysteries, Moralities, and Miracle-plays, which were at first performed in churches, and afterwards in the streets, on fixed or movable stages. For the most part, the Mysteries were founded on historic parts of the Old and New Testament, and the Miracle-Plays on the lives of the saints. . . . The moralities were plays in which the Virtues and Vices were personified. The earliest religious play which has been preserved is the *Christos Paschon* of Gregory Nazianzen, written in Greek, in the fourth century.¹⁴

Longfellow provides a helpful categorization for the types of Christian plays extant in the Middle Ages, and he names the *Christos Paschon*, which he has no qualms about attributing to Gregory, as the earliest of these plays. Given Longfellow's categorization, it seems that it would fit best as a late antique precursor to the medieval "Mystery" play. The two other types of medieval Christian drama—those that focus on the saints' lives and those that personify the virtues and vices—have their precursors among early Christian non-dramatic poems as well, in the hagiographic verse of Ambrose and Prudentius, and in the *Psychomachia* of Prudentius, respectively.

12. Longfellow, *Kavanagh*, 94.
13. Longfellow, *Kavanagh*, 66.
14. Longfellow, *Christus: A Mystery*, 444.

INTRODUCTION

Longfellow's *Golden Legend* contains a second interaction with the early Christian poets as well: early in the play, the protagonist, a German prince, visits a farmhouse in which a peasant family lives. He joins them for their evening prayers, and they sing a familiar evening hymn:

> O gladsome light
> Of the Father Immortal
> And of the celestial
> Sacred and blessed
> Jesus our Savior!
>
> Now to the sunset
> Again hast thou brought us;
> And seeing the evening
> Twilight we bless thee
> Praise thee, adore thee!
>
> Father omnipotent!
> Son, the Life-giver!
> Spirit, the Comforter!
> Worthy at all times
> Of worship and wonder![15]

This is Longfellow's translation of the ancient, third-century "*Phos Ilarion*" hymn. As Longfellow would have known, this hymn has been a staple of vespers services from the early Christian period through to the modern period—it is still sung today in eastern rite Catholic and Orthodox churches. Longfellow retains the short lines and three stanzas of the original, but extends each stanza to five lines, highlighting the potential for alliteration and rhyme between the short, dense phrases. Like Browning before him, Longfellow uses his considerable skill as a poet and translator to give his readers a version of early Christian poetry in nineteenth-century English, and cites the early Christian poets, especially Gregory, as founders of a tradition in which he is still writing 1,500 years later.

The model of Gregory's *Christos Paschon* seems to have stuck with Longfellow, and when he turned again to religious drama in

---

15. Longfellow, *Christus: A Mystery*, 168.

the early 1870s, he decided to write a tragedy based around the life of Christ. Unsurprisingly, he called this play *The Divine Tragedy*. While Longfellow saw Gregory's *Christos Paschon* as the founding work in the genre of Christian tragedy, he felt no compulsion to use either Gregory's main characters or Gregory's main narrative focus in his own play.

In *The Divine Tragedy*, Longfellow's blending of scriptural cento, paraphrase, and original verse is at times awkward and at times deeply moving. Judging by his journals and letters, *The Divine Tragedy* was a very important work to Longfellow, and he envisioned it as the first in a cycle of dramatic pieces. It would be followed by his *Golden Legend*, and third would come a pair of tragedies set in colonial New England. Together these plays were to form "a long and elaborate poem by the holy name of Christ; the theme of which would be the various aspects of Christendom in the Apostolic, Middle, and Modern Ages."[16] By the 1870s, Longfellow had written all the plays and he published them together as *Christus: A Mystery*. In subtitling the whole cycle "A Mystery," Longfellow called back to his 1850 note on the origins of Christian drama, wherein he characterized a mystery as focusing on the historical events of the scriptures, and the source of which he recognized, like Milton before him, as Gregory's *Christos Paschon*.

Longfellow, Browning, and Milton, then, stand as poets in whose imagination the Church Fathers—especially the Church Fathers' poems—were still alive and active, shaping their creative projects, at times prompting their admiring imitation, at times prompting intentional deviations or variations on what those early Christian poets established.

THE MODERN POETS AND THE FATHERS

With the passing of the Victorian age in literature, one might expect that any lingering interest in early Christian literature would die away, making way for a more secular, forward-looking

---

16. Longfellow, *Christus: A Mystery*, 7.

INTRODUCTION

modernity. But this was not to be the case, as can be seen in the interlinked interactions of T. S. Eliot and C. S. Lewis with the poetry of Prudentius. These interactions will be explored at length in a later essay in this book, but a brief summary of Eliot's debt to Prudentius is in order. In a November 1921 letter to his friend Richard Aldington, Eliot writes, "I imagine you dislike equally the Prudentianism of myself and Mr. Joyce, and expect you to abhor the poem on which I have been working and which I am taking with me!"[17] A year later, Eliot would write again to Aldington asking to borrow a copy of the Latin edition of Prudentius's poems. Finally, in his 1926 Clark Lectures, Eliot describes at length the superiority of Prudentius's hymns over those of the Victorians. Lest we think that Eliot's interest in Prudentius had no impact on his own poetry, we would do well to remember that the poem Eliot mentions working on in his letter to Aldington was, likely, *The Waste Land*.

From *Beowulf* to Milton, to Browning, to Longfellow, to T. S. Eliot we have travelled, and what has been the purpose of it all? Most importantly, I wish to have introduced to you a conversation. Major poets of the Anglo-American literary tradition have focused their time and talent upon the Church Fathers, some estimating them greater than the pagan classics, and some as lesser but still notable. All these poets have seen a continuity between the classical pagan, the early Christian, and the English literary tradition. All have had their work shaped by the Church Fathers of the Greek and Latin traditions. And all seem to say to us: what do you make of this? What do you make of the poets and the Fathers? What will you say of their relationship to one another? Browning explicitly asks in her essay: "What then should be done with our 'Fathers'? Leave them to perish by the time-Ganges, as old men innocent and decrepit, and worthy of no use or honor? Surely not. We may learn of them, if God will let us, love, and love is much."[18]

---

17. Eliot, *Letters*, 1:606.
18. Browning, *Essays*, 18.

2

Gregory Nazianzus and the Poetry of Orthodox Life

THIS ESSAY IS ABOUT two topics of great fascination for me, both as a scholar and as an Orthodox Christian: first, the ancient human practice of poetry, and second, the life and work of Saint Gregory Nazianzus, commonly called in the east Gregory the Theologian. With regard to the first topic, I am especially interested in how various cultures throughout human history have conceived of the operations of poetry in human life and culture. What exactly is a poem, and what does it do in culture? With regard to the second topic, I am especially interested in Gregory's conception of the life of Christian faithfulness as essentially sharing in the qualities of great poetry. To be interested in Gregory is, eventually, to be interested in poetry.

Gregory was born around AD 330 and died around AD 390. The sixty years of his life saw some of the most momentous shifts in Roman culture ever witnessed, in which some of the greatest minds and leaders of all time made their mark on history. Gregory himself was among the foremost of these minds, and to him and to his writings is due much of our knowledge and estimation of his age. Only his younger contemporary Augustine of Hippo could match him in sheer beauty of expression and felicity of thought. Gregory has earned for himself membership in the upper echelons of theological estimation: in the east he is one of only three Theologians of the Church, alongside the Apostle John and Symeon the New Theologian; Gregory is also one of the Three Holy Hierarchs, alongside Saints Basil and John Chrysostom. In the West, he is one of the Doctors of the Church, alongside such luminaries as Jerome, Augustine, and Thomas Aquinas.

If these accolades are not enough, here is the esteemed John McGuckin on the importance of Gregory:

> Byzantine Christianity, in a real sense, was Gregory's mind-child and masterpiece, partly by design, and partly by his transmission to later Byzantium as the last of the ancients and the first of their "moderns." He was the archetypal patron of the new Christian Byzantine culture that set out to clip the roses of Hellenism of their thorns and gather them in to decorate and color in the form of a New World order.[1]

Such a description might lead us to expect Gregory to be a very important, even self-important, man, a gold-cosseted and fine-mitered arch-doctrinaire, comforted by and comfortable in the halls of power. But, as is often the case in the lives of saints, when we look at the life of Gregory, we find a man suspicious and weary of position and power; he more than once literally ran from responsibility, and most of his life, he wanted a simple thing: to live and pray in solitude. But his life did not allow him much solitude, as he was continually pushed into prominent public positions, both to his own distress and to the benefit of the church and the commonwealth.

Let us indulge ourselves with one more quotation about Gregory, this time from the Victorian poet Elizabeth Barrett Browning:

> A noble and tender man was this Gregory, and so tender, because so noble; a man to lose no cubit of his stature for being looked at steadfastly, or struck at reproachfully. "You may cast me down," he said, "from my bishop's throne, but you cannot banish me from before God's."

---

1. McGuckin. *Saint Gregory of Nazianzus*, xxv.

> And bishop as he was, his saintly crown stood higher than his tiara, and his loving martyr-smile, the crown of a nature more benign than his fortune, shone up toward both . . . little did he care for bishoprics or high places of any kind,—the desire of his soul being for solitude, quietude, and that silent religion, which should "rather be than seem." But his father's head bent whitely before him, even in the chamber of his brother's death,—and Basil, his beloved friend, the "half of his soul," pressed on him with the weight of love; and Gregory feeling their tears upon his cheeks, did not count his own, but took up the priestly office. Poor Gregory! not merely as a priest, but as a man, he had a sighing life of it.[2]

Browning's read of Gregory is not too different from my own, as you will see, and we will return to her later in this essay.

It will be helpful to familiarize ourselves with the outline of Gregory's biography. In brief, Gregory was born to a wealthy family in Cappadocia; his father was also named Gregory and had converted to Christianity some years before young Gregory's birth. This conversion was largely due to the influence of Nonna, young Gregory's mother, who had been a Christian since birth. After his conversion, Gregory the Elder was ordained, and young Gregory grew up watching his father serve as a parish priest. Due in part to his family's considerable wealth and position, young Gregory was able to attend the finest schools in the world, first in Caesarea; then in Alexandria; and finally in Athens, at the famed Academy of Plato. At Athens Gregory would meet Basil the Great, who became Gregory's closest friend and would cause his deepest sorrow.

Returning to Cappadocia from Athens, both Basil and Gregory took the region by storm; they collaborated on theological anthologies, they designed schools and monasteries, and they became the hope for the future of Greek Christianity. But whereas Basil happily accepted first the priesthood and then the bishopric, Gregory wanted nothing more than to disappear into a life of solitary study and prayer. It was not to be. First the priesthood was foisted upon him by his father, then a new bishop position

---

2. Browning, *Essays*, 37–38.

was created for him by Basil. If he was reluctant but willing to be a priest, he was downright incensed at Basil's making him a bishop; Gregory accused his friend of worldly political machinations. He managed to shirk ministry until 379, when the hierarchs asked him to take charge of a small parish in Constantinople called Anastasia. It was there that Gregory took to the world's stage, preaching his five famous "Theological Orations" on the Trinity, being elected archbishop of Constantinople, and, finally, being appointed overseer of the first ecumenical council of Constantinople. But the infighting and posturing of bishops, emperors, and courtiers soured these positions in Gregory's heart, and he retired at the height of his career, seeking instead a life of solitary prayer, poetic composition, and pastoral counseling. Gregory died around AD 390, having paced the highest halls of academic, political, and ecclesial power, and having rejected it all, several times over.

I want to investigate Saint Gregory's life—and by extension the Orthodox Christian life in general—through looking at the poems that he spent so much of his life's effort in crafting. It is widely agreed upon that most of Gregory's poems were written in the last decade of his life, between his retirement from the episcopate in 381 and his death around 390. However, many of his shorter epigrams about his family and friends seem to have been written from time to time throughout his adult life. Take, for example, this poem about his mother, Nonna, who died in the middle of the liturgy, probably around AD 370:

> Weep all you mortals, of mortals the kin, but for those
> who are kin of
> Women like Nonna, who died while she prayed, I
> don't weep.[3]

This little poem is a polished gem of concision and verbal balance. It plays with two repeated terms, the first being the verb *weep* (*dakruo*), which appears as both the first word of the first line and the last word of the last line. Within this frame of weeping Gregory places the repeated word *mortal* (*thneitos*). Thus the poem hangs

---

3. Gregory Nazianzus, "Epigram 64." My translation.

on the verbal frame of *weep-mortals-mortals-weep*. But in between the second "mortals" and the second "weep," we have a note of difference: because of Nonna's pious death while praying, the speaker concludes that he will not weep. The repetitions are set off by the contrast of Nonna, who, by dying well, effectively undoes the weeping of those prone to death. All this is expressed in a tight metrical verse form called the elegiac couplet, which is a line of dactylic hexameter followed by a line of dactylic pentameter. In other words, the lines flow with the following rhythm, wherein – designates a long syllable and ∪ designates a short syllable:

– ∪ ∪ – ∪ ∪ – ∪ ∪ – ∪ ∪ – ∪ ∪ – ∪
– ∪ ∪ – ∪ ∪ – ∪ ∪ – ∪ ∪ – ∪

Gregory also plays with this standard rhythm with some variations of feet, according to classical Greek principles of prosody.

Now why would Gregory—celibate, grave, burdened with both hierarchical responsibility and the salvation of his soul—take the time to make a little poem like this? It may help to know that this is one of dozens of similar poems that he wrote about his mother. Simply put, Gregory regarded poetry as a cultural and spiritual practice with inherent ascetic value. You might say that, for Gregory, poetry was where aestheticism and asceticism met. More than that, it was in poetry that one could see that the aesthetic and the ascetic were, and had always been, united. It would be another sixteen hundred years before Dostoevsky would write that "Beauty will save the world."[4] But the concept is present in Gregory.

Gregory explicitly defends Christian participation in the cultural and literary education in his oration on Saint Basil the Great. He writes:

> I take it as admitted by men of sense, that the first of our advantages is education; and not only this our more noble form of it, which disregards rhetorical ornaments and glory, and holds to salvation, and beauty in the objects of our contemplation: but even that external culture

---

4. Dostoevsky, *Idiot*, 382.

which many Christians ill-judgingly abhor, as treacherous and dangerous, and keeping us afar from God. For as we ought not to neglect the heavens, and earth, and air, and all such things, because some have wrongly seized upon them, and honour God's works instead of God: but to reap what advantage we can from them for our life and enjoyment, while we avoid their dangers; not raising creation, as foolish men do, in revolt against the Creator, but from the works of nature apprehending the Worker, and, as the divine apostle says, bringing into captivity every thought to Christ: and again, as we know that neither fire, nor food, nor iron, nor any other of the elements, is of itself most useful, or most harmful, except according to the will of those who use it; and as we have compounded healthful drugs from certain of the reptiles; so from secular literature we have received principles of enquiry and speculation, while we have rejected their idolatry, terror, and pit of destruction. Nay, even these have aided us in our religion, by our perception of the contrast between what is worse and what is better, and by gaining strength for our doctrine from the weakness of theirs. We must not then dishonour education, because some men are pleased to do so, but rather suppose such men to be boorish and uneducated, desiring all men to be as they themselves are, in order to hide themselves in the general, and escape the detection of their want of culture.[5]

I want to call attention to Gregory's use of the term *beauty* in this passage. The noblest education, he writes, is concerned with "beauty in the objects of our contemplation." This beauty is higher than "rhetorical ornaments and glory." Now Gregory, due to his considerable Hellenic education, was very well versed in rhetoric and the ornamentation it required, as well as the glory one received for practicing oratory well. But rather than wholly contrasting secular learning with the study of salvation, Gregory sees secular learning as advantageous for "life and enjoyment." This is possible because education about "the works of nature" can teach us real truths,

5. Gregory Nazianzus, "Oration on Basil," 398–99.

both practical (for life) and aesthetic (for enjoyment). Though Gregory is clear that knowledge of salvation is a higher and more noble knowledge than that of "the heavens, and earth and air and all such things," there is a continuity—not an animosity—between such knowledges, as long as they are rightly understood. "Raising creation, as foolish men do, in revolt of the Creator," would be a misunderstanding of creation.

METERED POEMS, METERED SOULS

I want to turn now to the most theoretically important of Gregory's poems, "*Eis Ta Emmetra*," or "On the Metered," in which Gregory introduces his key idea linking the art of poetry to the life of Christian faithfulness. Gregory begins this poem, in characteristic style, with a complaint:

> I see the many penning, in this life of ours,
> A language that's unmetered.[6]

This opening remark contains an irony, for Gregory's description of the unmetered writing of the majority is written in a clear, regular iambic meter, which would have been recognized by his audience as the meter of conversation in Greek tragedy. This meter is called iambic trimeter, and is composed of three double iambic feet, totaling 12 syllables per line. We can illustrate the pattern of short and long syllables as follows:

$$U - U - U - U - U - U -$$

This sounds very different than the elegiac meter we met earlier. Gregory here uses the meter that tragic poets like Euripides or Sophocles would have used for serious men discussing serious matters, both debate of ideas and lament of misfortune. And lament he does:

> A language that's unmetered; they just let it flow
> And so erase each faded hour with their strained work

---

6. Gregory Nazianzus, "Eis Ta Emmetra," ll. 1–2.

> According none a blessing—it's all glottal waste.
> This kind of writing's only fit for tyrants' pens,
> Who fill their pages and their souls with passion's whims
> As sand spreads cross the shore, or Egypt swarmed with flies.
> Though such an art might please, it poisons human minds.
> We should not be so conquered, this I say: discard
> All words but those that God inspired and keep them close;
> Become, yourself, a harbor to hold back the storm.[7]

Gregory's language about unmetered writing is colorful: glottal waste, tyranny, poison. The second of these descriptors—namely, tyranny—is worth meditating on: Gregory, familiar with Plato's *Republic* as he was, knew that for the classical philosophers, the tyrant was the most disordered of men, unable to rule his appetites with reason, who thus dooms his own soul, and by extension, his city, to imbalance, injustice, and chaos.[8] Ever the good pastor, Gregory presents an alternative to the unmetered, tyrannical, popular writing: the scriptures themselves, the "God inspired" words. Later in the poem, he assures his audience that the scriptures are filled with the beauty of ordered language:

> Know this: there is much meteredness in Scripture too,
> As wise, old Rabbis of the Hebrew race confirm.[9]

But Gregory doesn't just want to recommend the reading of scripture as an alternative to trashy popular entertainment. He wants to provide a programme for the Christian who wants to write her own metered verses. He continues:

> But I have traveled, with my words, another road,
> And whether beautiful or not, I love it now—
> I set down my distress into each metered line[10]

Gregory's line "I set down my distress into each metered line" sums up well his overall poetics; in fact, I would say that it sums up two major elements of poetic theory across history.

---

7. Gregory Nazianzus, "Eis Ta Emmetra," ll. 3–12.
8. Plato meditates at length on the tyrannical soul in book 9 of *Republic*.
9. Gregory Nazianzus, "Eis Ta Emmetra," ll. 92–93.
10. Gregory Nazianzus, "Eis Ta Emmetra," ll. 22–24.

The Poets and the Fathers

Poetry, since the dawn of written literature, has always seemed caught between two purposes: the raw expression of human emotion, and the artful ordering of human language. These two elements can often seem opposed. If I want to rant about my concerns, to vent my troubles, I am not overly interested in careful patterns; I may even be drawn to create "glottal waste." And if I am interested in the artful ordering of human language, I will perhaps be wary of venting my distress: will not such expression overpower and wreck my careful craft? Better, perhaps, to choose more mundane, objective subjects. These conundrums often lead to two parallel types of literature: first, poems that are unartful, but accessible and stimulating, convulsions of feeling; and second, poems that are finely wrought, but ultimately boring and irrelevant, aesthetic objects. But Gregory would have distress set into metered lines; he would have the wildness of human feeling inhabit an ordered, linguistic space; would have that order lend structure and shape to the emotion.

In the next section, easily the most famous and debated passage of all of Gregory's poetry, he explains an approach to aesthetic form that is essentially spiritual and ascetic.

> Thus you may justly wonder why I write at all.
> With measured labor—first—I discipline my soul,
> For writing lines can order my unmetered mind,
> And keep my greedy pen in check—instead I spend
> My sweat on metric form.[11]

Over and over in these five and a half lines, Gregory repeats permutations of the Greek word *metron*: measured labor, unmetered mind, metric form. There is, first, the simple starting point of human nature: the unmetered mind, the soul plagued with and addicted to disorder. There is no measure in the human self, no disciplined rhythm of thought, feeling, or action. When the human can communicate, he does so with a greedy pen. We have already seen that such living and writing leads to tyranny, to being conquered by our own intemperance. Second, there is a way

---

11. Gregory Nazianzus, "Eis Ta Emmetra," ll. 33–37.

to begin to change that: namely, measured labor, working in an ordered way. This labor could take many different ascetic forms, but Gregory says he has chosen one: the metric form of poetry. Writing lines of poetry requires exact counting of syllables, precise, predetermined alternation of long and short syllables, and even rules for proper themes, subjects, and narrative or argumentative structures. These all combine to "keep [the] greedy pen in check." Gregory seems the type of person who struggles to restrain his tongue and his pen. He is not the over-hesitant man, suffering from lack of courage to speak. He is the cultural over-sharer, full of opinions, complaints, exhortations, and knows that poetry will allow him to speak, but only so much, only in certain ways, at certain times, on certain subjects. We could imagine someone with an opposite problem to Gregory being helped by poetry, too. If someone does not know what to say or how to say it, poetry gives a predetermined form to fill in with words, however halting, however hesitant. As we saw earlier, the worst kind of person is both loquacious and un-checked by form.

If we stopped here in the poem, poetry would appear to be something akin to physical exercise: it is difficult and rigorous and keeps us in shape, morally speaking. But Gregory wants to keep the concept of beauty close by:

> Second, I write for youths,
> And for whoever takes a deep delight in words.
> My verses read like sugar with elixir mixed;
> They can win men to virtue's work and discipline,
> By sweetening with art the bitterness of law.
> Think how a pulled-back bowstring loves to be let loose!
> At least my verse can satisfy your preferences
> For popular and lyric compositions. I
> Have written hymns and plays for those who wish to play,
> But not be hindered in their quest for Beauty.[12]

Delight, sugar, sweet, play: these words acknowledge the aesthetic joy of the poetic art, and ring familiar to us. A spoonful of sugar (that is, the beauty of poetry) makes the medicine (that is, virtue,

---

12. Gregory Nazianzus, "Eis Ta Emmetra," ll. 37–46.

discipline, law) go down. A playful poetry can both sweeten otherwise difficult moral truths, and also allow for seemingly un-ascetic activities like leisure and relaxation. And it allows for them in a way that does not ultimately divert the Christian audience from their overall spiritual work. Gregory characterizes this work as the quest for Beauty, capital B (the Greek root word here is *kalos*).

This passage has appeared to many readers somewhat trite. Do we really want to ascribe to a Mary Poppins understanding of art? Does this not reduce Christian art to window dressing—a harmless, irrelevant capitulation to the immaturity of "the youth" or "the populace"? More troubling, is this not an admission that there is no real, deep continuity between the aesthetic and the ascetic? I answer: this is why the first point is first. We have already seen that the demands of artistic form and craft have inherent moral and spiritual worth, and it is with this principle in mind that we can turn to the delights of poetry, because those delights were made possible by, even constituted of, the sweat-wrought form.

Gregory further clarifies the role of beauty in his next reason for writing:

> Third—
> And if this just sounds petty let me know—I write
> To win the current battle which we wage with words;
> Where each side seeks, through books, linguistic victory.
> (I speak of language that partakes in beauty, though
> Supremest Beauty is through contemplation reached.)[13]

Gregory admits that this reason may indeed be petty. And yet he acknowledges that in his age, just as in ours, there is a battle which is waged through words. He imagines that it is possible to bring our well-ordered, sweet-bitter poems to that battle, and find the upper hand. But Gregory is quick to clarify a hierarchy of goods. Language can partake in beauty—a very Platonic way of saying it—but there is a Beauty beyond language after which we quest, and that Beauty can and will be apprehended by the contemplating soul beyond language, beyond even discursive thought, when the

---

13. Gregory Nazianzus, "Eis Ta Emmetra," ll. 46–51.

mind acts as a purified eye, seeing the light that is God Himself in his self-revealing, with which He illuminates all who diligently seek Him. Though Gregory is not explicit about this in the poem, he is in his Theological Orations:

> What God is in nature and essence, no man ever yet has discovered or can discover. . . . In my opinion it will be discovered when that within us which is godlike and divine, I mean our mind and reason, shall have mingled with its Like, and the image shall have ascended to the Archetype, of which it has now the desire. And this I think is the solution of that vexed problem as to "We shall know even as we are known." But in our present life all that comes to us is but a little effluence, and as it were a small effulgence from a great Light.[14]

Like his fellow Cappadocians and the later hesychasts of the medieval era, Gregory emphasizes both the unknowability of God's essence, and the real possibility of participatory union in God's energy. Far from denigrating the role of the mind in spiritual experience, Gregory clarifies the proper use of the mind in the Christian life, namely the contemplation of divine Beauty. He also clarifies that earthly language can participate in beauty, and this beauty is not of a different origin than the divine; it is, in Gregory's words, "a small effulgence from a great Light." There is, therefore, no such thing as a beauty disconnected from the divine. There is only the miserable human disregard for the divine source of all earthly beauty.

Maybe this has all seemed overly theoretical. Gregory knows this, perhaps, and he turns his attention in the next section to the realities of mortal life:

> And fourth, when winter wind brings sickness, struggle, death,
> My poems comfort me, swan-like old man; they lull
> Me with their wings, embolden me like woodwind hymns—
> No threnodies, but songs to lead me ever on.[15]

---

14. Gregory Nazianzus, "Second Theological Oration," 294.
15. Gregory Nazianzus, "Eis Ta Emmetra," ll. 52–54.

Let us remember the context of this poem: Gregory is in the final decade of his life; as we will see later, he had been through some of the most grueling personal and professional experiences of his age; when Gregory says "sickness, struggle, death," he knows of what he speaks. He had by this time buried—and written beautiful orations and poems for—his brother, his sister, both parents, and his best friend. Gregory, in a real sense, had outlived everyone he loved, save Gregory of Nyssa. He seems to have felt alone at the end of an age, and looked to poetry for comfort, for new courage, for a music in time with which he could exit the stage of history, not in despair, but in hope. Art has been for many a stay against death, a rage against the dying of the light. But Gregory sees it as both a consolation for mortality and preparation for the journey of the afterlife.

In this fourth and final reason for writing poetry, Gregory has taken us back to the first reason in a transformed way. If his first reason has to do with the discipline of the soul in this life, then the fourth reason has to do with the discipline of the soul in the face of the next life. It is possible, further, to discern concentric circles of concern in these four reasons: at the center is the ascetic activity of the individual soul, the first reason. One circle larger is the education and entertainment of the Christian community, the second reason. The third, wider circle, is the general discourse of culture, including, but not limited to, the Church. And finally, there is the fourth reason, which concerns itself with the widest (and, paradoxically, most central) context of all: mortal and immortal life.

There is much more that can be said about Gregory's attitude toward poetics in particular and culture-creation in general. For our purposes it is enough to say that Gregory manages to avoid the trap of myopia that most theories of art and culture fall into. Our age, for instance, is trapped between two competing visions of art: first an anemic romanticism that revels in undisciplined self-expression, and, second, an anxious dogmaticism that demands adherence to some cultural and political party line, deriving art's worth wholly from the purity of its dogma—not its craft, beauty, or earnest feeling. Gregory agrees both that art is self-expressive and that it can become involved in culture wars, but he does not reduce art to either. And the essentially ascetic, formally robust nature of his first reason establishes that formal and moral rigor are prerequisites for any art that would seek to express emotion, teach truth, or battle rival philosophies. The intemperate human writing disordered poetry thus disqualifies themselves from any proper use of that art.

THE ADVENTURE OF DOCTRINE

In the previous section I summarized what I believe to be an essential element in Saint Gregory's understanding of the Christian life; that is, that the ascetic work necessary for the healing of the human soul is akin to the disciplined crafting of formal Greek poetry. Thus the crafting of poetry—and by extension any formal, creative endeavor—can become a part of one's spiritual ascesis. Further, we saw that such disciplined ascetic practice, whether poetic or not, is necessary to prepare one to become a winsome teacher of truth, a defender of the faith in a pluralistic public square, and, ultimately, a human who can face death with courage.

I now want to turn to a rather different sort of poem, in which we see Gregory in the second and third modes; that is, as teacher of truth and refuter of error. If Gregory's famous five Theological Orations are his most important theological work in prose, then his most important theological work in verse is his series of poems on the Trinity, commonly called the *Poemata Arcana*. These poems have a close affinity with the Theological Orations and often summarize his central points in those orations. But the overall project of the *Poemata Arcana* is deeply embedded in the classical poetic tradition. In his opening poem, "On the Father," Gregory writes:

> Knowing that here we are crafting a raft to accomplish an arduous
> Voyage, or delicate feathers to rocket to stars in the heavens,
> Daring to show, to illumine in language the nature of godhead
> (Even the heavenly creatures lack power to render due praise), to
> Scan the divinity's fathomless boundary, and helm of all being[16]

16. Gregory Nazianzus, "On the Father," ll. 1–5. My translation.

The Poets and the Fathers

In classical Greek epic, it was expected that the poet would do several things in his opening lines: first, he would write in dactylic hexameter: – ∪ ∪ – ∪ ∪ – ∪ ∪ – ∪ ∪ – ∪ ∪ – ∪. Second, he would state his theme at the outset, and that theme would be ambitious, world-spanning, concerning both men and gods, and often, though not always, relating to the journey of a hero. Gregory meets all these expectations in his opening lines. We see not the iambic meter of the "*Eis Ta Emmetra*," but the full dactylic hexameter of Homer. We are also introduced to an epic theme: "to illumine in language the nature of godhead." And we have the requisite epic journey: "an arduous voyage," an adventure "to stars in the heavens."

I admit that my use of the term *rocket* in my translation can appear anachronistic. It certainly is if we take *rocket* to imply a certain space age technology; but if we think of astronautics in its more romantic sense—to rise, on whatever technology (a divine chariot perhaps?) into the heavens, to become literal star-sailors—this accords with the sense of Gregory's words. If literal astronautical exploration is extremely difficult and prohibitively costly in our own day, it was nearly unthinkable, unimaginable, in Gregory's day. But I say *nearly*, because Gregory would have known several accounts of astronauts from classical tradition, most especially from Plato, who imagines that pre-incarnate souls are led around the heavens by the gods, and learn heavenly mysteries that they will subsequently forget when they are incarnated in bodies.[17] Gregory would also have likely known the poems of Parmenides, Hesiod, Lucretius, and Ovid, who depict both mystic visions and literal journeys through the planets, the stars, and the divine realms beyond them.

Gregory admits and wrestles with the audacity of his task, but ultimately gives an apologetic for his attempt:

> Nevertheless it is often more pleasing to God to receive gifts
> Not from the affluents' fingers, but out of the lack of the loving.
> Therefore with boldness I break into speech; but flee to a distance

17. This heavenly journey is depicted in Plato's *Phaedrus*, secs. 247–48.

> If you are one of the wicked; my word is for those who are pure,
> or
> Those who are set on the pathway of purification.[18]

There are two prerequisites for attempting to speak of the godhead: first, a poor and humble spirit that honestly loves God. And second, a soul that has been or is being purified by the life of ascesis. This mention of purification especially connects this poem to Gregory's first Theological Oration. In it, he writes:

> Discussion of theology ... is not for all people, but only for those who have been tested and have found a sure footing in study, and, more importantly, have undergone, or at the very least are undergoing, purification of body and soul. For one who is not pure to lay hold of pure things is dangerous, just as it is for weak eyes to look at the sun's brightness.[19]

In his prose oration, Gregory emphasizes the strengthening power of ascesis: those who are not at least undergoing purification are not strong enough to consider God's nature. They will be blinded, like Plato's character who, after a lifetime in the shadows, stumbles for the first time into broad daylight.[20] Speaking of Plato, Gregory also clarifies that study and testing are also prerequisites for discussion of theology. It is curious that he does not mention study in the poem; what is most important there is the "pathway of purification." This should not surprise us, given the amount of time he spends on the need for metered-ness in the "*Eis Ta Emmetra.*" In all, it takes a special kind of poet to be able to write about God; it takes a poet who is spiritually "in shape," purified, bold, and willing to suffer the buffets that all epic heroes must: waves, monsters, shipwrecks, the thunderclaps of angry gods.

After a few more lines warning against the dangers of wickedness, Gregory performs another convention of the classical epic tradition, calling on the muse:

---

18. Gregory Nazianzus, "On the Father," ll. 6–10. My translation.
19. Gregory Nazianzus, "First Theological Oration," 285.
20. See Plato, *Rep.* 7.

The Poets and the Fathers

> Now may the spirit of God re-enliven my mind and my language;
> Make them a mustering orchestra tuned to the truth so that all men
> Join in rejoicing, united together in spirit with Godhead.[21]

We could compare this to Homer's opening lines of the Odyssey:

> Tell me, my Muse, of the cleverest man, of his many devices,
> Pilgrim diverted by waves and by wind from his homeward endeavor,
> After he toppled the god-blessed towers of Trojans.[22]

Whereas Homer calls on the pagan muse Kaliope to help him sing of Odysseus, the man of many devices, Gregory calls on the Holy Spirit to aid him in singing of God. Gregory was not, in fact, the first to do this; we have the example of at least two Latin Christian epic poets before him, Juvencus and Proba. Still, Gregory may have been the first to do it in Greek, and, together with Juvencus and Proba, he set the standard for Christian epic forever afterward, influencing everyone from the fifth-century poet Nonnus of Panopolis to much later poets like Dante and, especially, Milton. But we are concerned here less with poetic tradition and more with how Gregory uses the language of poetry to help us conceive of the spiritual life: if ascetic endeavor is like the organization of language into meter, then the attempt to think and speak about the Trinity is like an epic journey: both truly perilous and truly worthwhile.

The next step is to speak of the Godhead:

> Lo, there is only one God, without source, without cause, without limit
> Set by a being preceding him, nor by a being succeeding him,
> Aeon-encompassing, infinite God, and the Father of Jesus,[23]

Given that his audience would be made up of both Greek Christians and Greek pagans, Gregory uses the language of the Greek philosophical tradition to clarify the nature of God the Father. He

---

21. Gregory Nazianzus, "On the Father," ll. 22–24. My translation.
22. Homer, *Odyssey*, ll. 1–3. My translation.
23. Gregory Nazianzus, "On the Father," ll. 25–27. My translation.

has no source, cause, or limit; meaning that He is the source, He the first cause, He the limit of all other beings—indeed, perhaps even of being itself. This language may seem obvious to us, but it is a radical statement within a poem posed as an epic. Epics deal with imperfect humans and arguably even more imperfect gods. Hesiod, in his seventh century BC *Theogony* had given a very different account of divinity than Gregory:

> Celebrate in song first of all the revered race of the gods
> from the beginning, those whom Earth and wide Heaven begot,
> and the gods sprung of these, givers of good things.
> Then next, the goddesses sing of Zeus,
> the father of gods and men, as they begin and end their strain,
> how much he is the most excellent among the gods and supreme in power.[24]

In the very title of his epic, *Theogony*—literally, the birth of the gods—Hesiod sets us up to expect that gods by their very nature are not without source or cause. Hesiod explicitly states that heaven and earth begot the gods, of whom Zeus is the most powerful, the most worthy of worship. We also learn later that Earth and Heaven themselves were preceded by Night and Day, and, before them, Chaos. But even Chaos, Hesiod writes, "came to be." For Gregory, "came to be" is not applicable to God at all, for no beings precede Him. Effectively, Gregory has leaped beyond and before the whole of Greek epic imagination, and dropped us at the utmost east of being, where no mythologies adhere. And here, he says, is where our adventure will begin—not in burning Troy or yearning Rome, but here—before and beyond all beings, where high fantasy leaves off, and we stand before utter mystery, hoping for the One beyond being to reveal Himself to us. Reveal Himself He does, and what is revealed is Trinity:

> Aeon encompassing, God, and the Father of Jesus
> He who is Lord and the only Begotten. Mistaken are claims that the

---

24. Hesiod, *Theogony*, ll. 45–50.

> Father experienced bodily suffering. Mind cannot suffer.
> One there is too who is God, in one Godhead with Father: the Logos,
> Living impression of God who is Father. And none but the Son have been
> Born from origin-less One—a Uniqueness from Who is Unique—
> Equal in power, the Father remaining the parent while Son is
> Authoring worlds and all laws, strength and the mind of the Father.
> Spirit of God there is also, the God out of God who is mighty.

For those who know Gregory's prose writings about the Trinity, these lines are particularly impressive inasmuch as they demonstrate Gregory's ability to maneuver complex philosophical language about the persons of the Trinity into perfect dactylic hexameter. First, God exists as Father. The one who the Father begets is the Son, and the Son is the only begotten of the Father. This Son is God, is in one Godhead with the Father, and has equal power with Him. The Son is Logos, the Word of God. And He is the one who authors all worlds and laws.

Many of these descriptions of the Son and his relationship with the Father come from John 1: "In the beginning was the Word, and the Word was with God and the Word was God. . . . All things were made by him and without him was not anything made that was made."[25] Gregory is also being true to the language of the Council of Nicaea, which proclaimed, in AD 324, that Christians believe "in one Lord Jesus Christ, the Son of God, begotten of the Father, [the only-begotten; that is, of the essence of the Father, God of God,] Light of Light, very God of very God, begotten, not made, consubstantial with the Father."[26]

Finally, Gregory also gives us a brief description of the Spirit: "God out of God who is mighty." This language, though brief, is also in accordance with the New Testament and the ecumenical councils, for Christ describes the Spirit in the Gospel of John as

---

25. John 1:1, 3 (KJV).
26. Leith, *Creeds of the Churches*, 30–31.

"the Spirit of Truth which proceedeth from the Father."[27] Further, the Council of Constantinople, in which Gregory took part, declared that the spirit is "the Lord and Giver of Life, who proceeds from the Father, who is worshipped and glorified together with the Father and the Son, who spoke by the prophets."[28] Admittedly, Gregory is summing up a lot with those few words "God out of God." Nevertheless, he is right to highlight the Godhood of the Spirit, if for no other reason than that he has already stated that we are about to encounter the Godhead, and the most important thing to affirm about the Spirit is that he is God, and comes from God the Father. Those desiring a more robust account of the Holy Spirit need only to look to a later poem in the *Poemata Arcana* titled "On the Spirit," which explicates the doctrine of the Holy Spirit in 93 lines of verse.

Gregory's recasting of the subject of Christian poetry—and indeed of Christian life—is as important to his thought as is his recasting of the Christian poet as one who purifies oneself through the ascesis of literary creation. The subject of poetry can, of course, be any earthly thing, but at its height, poetry has the power—if only barely—to sing the Godhead. And this was no impractical subject for Gregory. For he lived through at least three great theological controversies, first the lingering Arian controversy, inherited from the previous generation; then the Julian controversy of his early career; and finally the Eunomian controversy at his career's end. All three of these controversies are addressed and clarified by Gregory's *Poemata Arcana*.

The Arian heresy had beset the church in the early 320s, soon after the legalization of Christianity under Constantine. Arius had claimed that Christ was a created being, that there was a time when he was not, and that his nature was similar to the Father's, but certainly not the same. The Council of Nicaea, and Gregory's reiteration of it in his poetry, is clearly anti-Arian. In being so it is also anti-Eunomian, for Eunomius was something of a neo-Arian, casting doubt on the Son's divinity, but also dismissing the Spirit's

---

27. John 15:26 (KJV).
28. Leith, *Creeds of the Churches*, 33.

divinity. Gregory's unabashed trinitarianism thus clarifies his stance, and what he wants his reader's stance to be, on both major controversies.

There was, however, a more insidious controversy that took place in the 360s. This was the persecution of the Church by Emperor Julian the Apostate, whose acquaintance both Gregory and Basil had made at the Academy in Athens. Julian rejected the Christianity of the Constantinian dynasty and attempted to erect a new pagan regime. As part of this neo-pagan revival, Julian attempted to ban Christians from teaching the Greek classics. Julian argued that because Christians did not believe in the pagan gods, it was hypocritical of them to try to teach about, say, Homer or Virgil, who did believe in the gods. Christians should only teach books that they believed in, and this disqualified them from being classical educators. Such an argument was especially frustrating to the classically-minded Gregory, who saw himself as a rightful inheritor of the Greek classics, even as he rejected their polytheism. In borrowing the epic meter, epic structure, epic invocation of the muse, and epic theme, Gregory is showing what he thinks of Julian's reasoning: the classical epic is most definitely the Christian's inheritance. Christians will use it, Christians may even improve on it, even as the Christian God is supreme above the petty classical pantheon. In his response to the Julian controversy as well as the Arian and Eunomian controversies, we see Gregory's earlier third reason for writing at play: to win the battle that we wage with words.

AT THE CORNER OF FAME AND ETERNITY

In the end, human renown did not so much matter to Gregory the Theologian. And it is an irony of history that he is now one of the most quoted, most praised, most—simply put—famous of all the Church Fathers. You will find his name not just in the tomes of Orthodox Theological history, but in the works of John Milton, Henry Wadsworth Longfellow, John Henry Newman, and, as we saw before, Elizabeth Barrett Browning. Poets tend to not only praise him as a poet, and to translate his poetry, but to include Gregory in their own original poetry. Elizabeth Barrett Browning mentions him in two passages of her sonnets. The first passage appears in her sonnet on the blindness of her beloved mentor Hugh Stuart Boyd:

> Still seeing, to sounds of softly-turned book-leaves,
> Sappho's crown-rose, and Meleager's Spring,
> And Gregory's starlight on Greek-burnished eves:
> Till Sensuous and Unsensuous seemed one thing,
> Viewed from one level,—earth's reapers at the sheaves
> Scarce plainer than Heaven's angels on the wing.[29]

Here Gregory is reckoned with the pagan poets Sappho and Meleager, quite a famous trio indeed. When Hugh Stuart Boyd died, Browning wrote another poem for him, which also mentions Gregory:

> Three gifts the Dying left me,—Aeschylus,
> And Gregory Nazianzen, and a clock
> Chiming the gradual hours out like a flock
> Of stars whose motion is melodious.
> The books were those I used to read from, thus
> Assisting my dear teacher's soul to unlock
> The darkness of his eyes; now, mine they mock,
> Blinded in turn by tears; now, murmurous
> Sad echoes of my young voice, years agone
> Intoning from these leaves the Grecian phrase,
> Return and choke my utterance. Books, lie down
> In silence on the shelf there, within gaze;
> And thou, clock, striking the hour's pulses on,
> Chime in the day which ends these parting days![30]

Whereas in the previous poem, Gregory had been listed among lyric poets (Sappho and Meleager), he is now in the company of the first great Greek tragedian, Aeschylus. This tragic turn is appropriate, for this is a poem of mourning. Further, the themes of fame and eternity are wound within this poem. The clock, which

29. Browning, *Poems*, 437.
30. Browning, *Poems*, 438.

accompanies Aeschylus and Gregory, is the repeated reminder of both the continuance and the end of time. Browning's grief for Boyd, with whom she had completed some of the first English translations of Gregory's shorter poems, is wrapped up with her grief for all the vanished past, both hers and that of Aeschylus and Gregory. These passings are described as "parting days" which the clock measures. And yet, in Browning's Christian imagination, there will be some future "day which ends these parting days," when death and time will cease, and reunion with all that is lost will be possible.

We can see Gregory's own outlook on the human tension between the loss of this life and the hope of eternity in his heartbreaking epigrams on Basil. As we saw before, Basil was his best friend, who had deeply wounded Gregory by forcing him to become a bishop. Gregory considered this not only a breach of trust, but also a misuse of clerical power. And yet, after Basil died, Gregory wrote the following epigram in his honor:

> Sooner the body divides from the soul while alive, than we sunder,
>   Oh Basil, servant of Christ, from each other I once thought.
> Now I am suffering, sundered, as destined. If only you lifted me,
>   Set me again alongside you in heavenly chorus!
> Never abandon me, never—oh swear by this tomb! For I will not
>   Leave it, not willingly: this is your Gregory's promise.[31]

In these lines we have a variation on one of Gregory's favorite images of friendship: one soul in two bodies. Or, to speak more precisely, one friend is the body and the other is the soul. Sundering body from soul while alive is as unnatural as sundering Gregory and Basil from one another. And yet, Gregory finds himself so torn. Instead of merely lamenting, or, worse, chiding Basil for past slights, Gregory invokes the glorified Basil: "If only you lifted me!" Gregory is wishing not quite for death here, but just to be beside his friend again, glorified as angels. Then, in the final lines, he returns to earth, presenting a shadow of togetherness. Since Gregory cannot be with Basil's soul, he will stay by his friend's tomb, and,

---

31. Gregory Nazianzus, "Epigram 2: On Basil," ll. 1–6. My translation.

by implication, his body. He will serve the long vigil of earthly grief, which only ends in death. And he asks for Basil's presence, and perhaps, his prayers: "Never abandon me." Though this poem has little bitterness in it, and no resentment, it is still, perhaps, an invitation for Basil to again prove his loyalty. Though he was inconstant in life, Basil may make up for it in eternity.

In closing, let us turn to the final lines of Gregory's masterful poem "Concerning His Own Life." This very long poem retells Gregory's whole biography, which we summarized at the beginning of this essay: how he received the best education in the late antique world; how he was ordained priest, then bishop, and, finally, archbishop of Constantinople, installed in splendor by the emperor himself; then how he gave up all his worldly power and is glad to be rid of it. Gregory brings his poem to a close with a flourish of paradox:

> I've ended as a dead man who is living still,
> The well-defeated one who, in a wonder, won:
> For all I'm left with is my God and godly friends,
> And neither thrones nor fame which ever fragments.[32]

Gregory has lost all things men praise, and he is thankful for it. For he has the only substantial things: God and godly friends. No throne, no acclaim, are worth those things. It is hard to get more famous than Gregory—famous in Athens, in Cappadocia, in Constantinople, in all the Roman world—but, except perhaps for his youthful fame in Athens, Gregory considers all his fame to be suffering, all his power to be pain. Here are his final words in the poem:

> Unto the Church what I can give are tears....
> Where will my life complete its run? Oh Logos, say:
> I wish to find that final Home immovable,
> Where God—triune and all-united brightness—dwells
> The light divine, whose glimmered image lifts us up.[33]

32. Gregory Nazianzus, "Concerning His Own Life," ll. 1919–22. My translation.

33. Gregory Nazianzus, "Concerning His Own Life," ll. 1943, 1946–49. My translation.

I like to think Gregory's poems are his tears, but they are also more: they are the meters of a meter-loving man. A man quick to rage, quick to defend himself, quick to retreat from responsibility, even from having, sometimes, to talk to anyone. He is as much *philometron* as he is *philo-sopher*. For the philosopher is one who would love to be wise, would love to mingle with wisdom, and yet who knows he is not there yet. And Gregory desires to be unmoved, well-metered, but knows he has lines and stanzas to go before he gets there; and so do we all, illumined by faint glimmers like candle-flame from icon-gold, reach toward our unshakable home, where dwell Wisdom and Temperance in Beauty forever.

3

The Sweetened List

The Strange Case of Saint Gregory Nazianzus's Poem on the Biblical Canon

SOON AFTER ATHANASIUS WROTE his famous letter about the biblical canon in 367, the Cappadocian orator, poet, and bishop Gregory Nazianzus wrote a poem on the same subject. Though his poem "On the Genuine Books of the God-Breathed Writings" has not been treated as possessing the same authority as Athanasius's letter, Gregory's poem holds an important place in the history of the formulation of the canon in the fourth century.[1] However, this poem is not only useful for Gregory's list and its idiosyncrasies, but, inasmuch as it is canon-list-as-lyric-poem, it is illustrative of Gregory's unique approach to theological debate and education through the medium of literary art. Through a close reading of the poem and a comparison to the canon lists found in Eusebius and Athanasius, I argue that Gregory's poem transcends mere list-making and becomes a testing ground for a central, contested theme in Gregory's poetics.

Most of Gregory's poetry was written in the 380s, between his retirement from the episcopate of Constantinople in 381 and his death around 389. A few of these poems—especially "On

---

1. Gregory Nazianzus, *On God and Man*, 7.

Virginity," "On the Metered," and "On His Own Life"—have long been of interest to modern scholars. "On the Genuine Books of the God-Breathed Writing" is relatively short, only 39 lines compared to over 1,900 in "On his Own Life." Still, Brian Dunkle has argued, it serves as an introduction to all of Gregory's poems on scriptural themes and stories.[2] The poem is broken up into three parts: in the first eight lines Gregory presents a theology of scripture in miniature. In the next 21 lines, he presents his canon list of the Old Testament. Finally, in the last ten lines, he presents his canon list of the New Testament. In both lists, from time to time, he includes pithy descriptions of the book or its author.

Here are the opening lines, rendered by Gregory in dactylic dexameter:

> Turn to the writings divine with your tongue and your mind—turn always.
> God is rewarding to those who engage in this feat and its toil,
> Kindling for us a glow to illumine the hidden, the best things,
> So to be goaded by holiest Deity's lofty commandments.
> Thirdly, be led in your mind from the troubles of earthly dominions
> So that your soul will remain unabducted by alien volumes,
> (Many the passages there that are sown with instructions of evil).
> Take, then, beloved, this number, the only that I can approve of.[3]

Gregory's meter here is that of the Greek epics and of the didactic verse of the Latin poets like Horace. But his content is an enumeration of the benefits of reading Scripture: first, he promises that God rewards those who read scripture (and reading here involves both the contemplating mind and the articulating tongue). The reward is an illumination, however brief, of hidden and best things. God reveals not just practical but arcane knowledge to the scripture reader. Second, scripture reveals the commandments of

---

2. Gregory Nazianzus, *Poems on Scripture*, 25.

3. Gregory Nazianzus, "On the Genuine Books of the God-Breathed Writing," ll. 1–8. My translation.

The Sweetened List

God that can and should motivate right action in the reader. This motivation is described in Gregory's Greek as *nuttesthai*, a sharp physical object, a prick, nail, or goad. Third, Gregory says that through scripture the mind of the reader can ascend past earthbound cares and beyond books that have evil teaching inserted into them. This worry throws into sharp relief the importance of the rest of the poem: if Gregory or his reader gets the canon list wrong, they will be searching out, goaded by, and led up into erroneous teachings. This, then, is Gregory's very practical theology of scripture reading: through scripture God fulfills the human desire to learn hidden things, provides humans with motivation for right action, and leads the human mind away from low and erroneous things to dwell on pure and heavenly matters.

Next, Gregory turns to the Old Testament:

> Now of historical volumes permit only twelve of them total,
> These tell eldest of things, things wise Hebrews believe.
> First there is Genesis, Exodus next, and Leviticus.
> The book of Numbers next, then Deuteronomy.
> The book of Joshua, then Judges. Ruth comes eighth.
> Next are the acts of the Kings—the ninth and the tenth
>   of the volumes,
> Chronicles afterward. Last, Ezra you must possess too.[4]

In this list of the first twelve books of the Old Testament, Gregory is freewheeling, to say the least, with meter. The first line is a standard line of dactylic hexameter. But then Gregory downshifts into heavily augmented lines of both dactylic pentameter and iambic trimeter (the standard line of Athenian tragedy, which he favors in other poems). Finally, in the lines about Kings, Chronicles, and Ezra, he pulls back into dactylic hexameter, albeit liberally augmented. I have tried to retain these augmentations as much as possible, in the English. Why does Gregory begin to mix his meters here? The metrical structure of the Hebrew book names seems to have led him to adapt the meter of his lines to suit them. For example, the Greek transliteration *deuteros nomos* is an unforgiving

---

4. Gregory Nazianzus, "On the Genuine Books of the God-Breathed Writing," ll. 9–15. My translation.

phrase that can only fit well, if at all, into an iambic or trochaic line, not a dactylic one. *Basileion* on the other hand—the word for the books of Kings—fits best at the end of a dactylic line given its structure. Thus, Gregory's choice of mixed meters for the sections listing the books was something of a formal necessity.

Let us continue to look at Gregory's list of Old Testament books:

> And then in lines of verse five books: the first of Job,
> The next by David, then three Solomonic books:
> Ecclesiastes, Song of Songs, and Proverbs next.
> Then five of equal rank: the spirit-filled prophetic books.
> Indeed there is one text made from all twelve of these:
> Hosea, and then Amos, Micah is the third;
> The book of Joel, then Jonah, Obadiah next,
> And Nahum then, Habbakuk then, and Zephaniah.
> The last are Haggai, Zachariah, Malachi:
> And these are one. The second is Isaiah's book.
> Then that of Jeremiah—he was called from birth.
> Ezekiel's writing then, and Daniel, graceful one.
> Certainly now I have numbered the twenty-two books of antiquity
> To match the number of the Hebrew Alphabet.[5]

Gregory's list here, largely in iambic trimeter, matches rather precisely the second-century list of Melito as recorded by Eusebius.[6] Both, for example, exclude Esther. Gregory's list is also in agreement with Athanasius for the most part, though Athanasius includes Lamentations, the letter of Jeremiah, and Baruch with the book of Jeremiah, and Gregory does not clarify what he would include under Jeremiah's writing.

Where Gregory arguably diverges most from the canon lists of Eusebius and Athanasius is in his section on the New Testament:

> And number with me now the newer mystery:
> Matthew: he wrote to the Hebrews the wonders of Messias.

---

5. Gregory Nazianzus, "On the Genuine Books of the God-Breathed Writing," ll. 16–29. My translation.

6. See Eusebius, *History of the Church*, 4.26.

Mark wrote for Italy, Luke to the Hellenists.
John wrote to all men, herald of greatness, the heavenly pilgrim.
And next the Acts of wise apostles of the Lord.
From Paul the four plus ten epistles are placed next,
Seven the Catholic epistles, the first one by James.
Then two by Peter, three from that same John once more.
And Jude's is number seven. All are in your grasp.
And as for books outside these, none are genuine.[7]

Obviously missing from this list is the Apocalypse, or Revelation, which Athanasius includes, and Eusebius tentatively treats as genuine. Why is the Apocalypse missing, especially in a canon list as late as the 380s, when Athanasius's 367 letter, and Pope Damasus's council of Rome in 382 seem to have established it? Frank Thielmann recently argued that Gregory may indeed include the Apocalypse of John obliquely in his poem. He writes: "It is possible that Gregory intended his reference to John as one who entered heaven to cover the Apocalypse. . . . If it refers to the Apocalypse, [it] agrees with an ancient order of the New Testament books that placed the Apocalypse directly after the gospels."[8] To further bolster this reading, Thielman points out that elsewhere in his writings, Gregory treats the Apocalypse as a genuine work of the apostle John.

Making Gregory's possible exclusion of the Apocalypse more curious is his inclusion of 2 Peter, 2 and 3 John, and Jude, on which Eusebius, some decades before, had suspended judgment. Still, in including these sometimes contested books, Gregory is in the company of Athanasius and his Western contemporaries.

THE CANON LIST AND "ON THE METERED"

The idiosyncrasies of Gregory's list make it an interesting addition to the canon lists of the mid- to late-fourth century, but of less importance to the development of the canon than Athanasius's

---

7. Gregory Nazianzus, "On the Genuine Books of the God-Breathed Writing," ll. 30–39. My translation.

8. Thielman, "Place of Apocalypse," 156.

letter. Arguably, the ongoing significance of Gregory's list lies in its form. None of the three canon list makers mentioned so far—Melito, Eusebius, or Athanasius—wrote their lists in such a way as to make the lists themselves works of art. Gregory did. Lest we doubt Gregory's intentions in writing the list as a poem, let us turn to Gregory's oft referenced poem "On the Metered":

> I write for youths,
> And for whoever takes a deep delight in words.
> My verses read like sugar with elixir mixed;
> They can win men to virtue's work and discipline
> By sweetening with art the bitterness of law.[9]

The subjects of Gregory's poems are often theological teaching and biblical interpretation. Gregory describes these subjects metaphorically here as "elixir" and "bitter . . . law." The art of verse is the sugar and the sweetness that wins readers to virtue and discipline. Brian Dunkle has argued that for Gregory's Greek audience, the sweetness would lie in both ease of memorization and literary allusion: "Following the established method of didactic verse, these poems incorporate certain ornaments to make them more pleasant. In this way, Gregory sprinkles his verse with delicate linguistic markers that encourage . . . familiarity with classical learning, so central to Gregory's own formation."[10] Thus Gregory's canon list fits as much into the classical poetic tradition stretching back to Homer as it does the conversation about the biblical canon. In employing the poetic lines of Homeric epic and Athenian tragedy to speak of scripture, Gregory is raising the subject of biblical canon into the hallowed company of the fall of Troy and the sufferings of Oedipus.

Unsurprisingly, this endeavor has rankled some critics. D. A. Sykes has lamented Gregory as a writer of "tedious . . . mnemonic verse."[11] Joannes Quasten, too, writes that Gregory's didactic po-

---

9. Gregory Nazianzus, "Eis Ta Emmetra," ll. 37–41.
10. Gregory Nazianzus, *Poems on Scripture*, 22.
11. Gregory Nazianzus, *Poemata Arcana*, 58.

etic project often produces "nothing more than prose in meter."[12] Though he praises Gregory's "historical and autobiographical poems," Quasten admits that Gregory "could not be called an inspired poet."[13] This preference for autobiographical verse over didactic verse is much in line with the last 200 years of critical preferences in the West. But didactic verse has waxed and waned in favor throughout history: in the early eighteenth century, for example, Alexander Pope praises the poet not for originality or pouring out his heart, but in writing verse containing "what oft was thought, but ne'er so well expressed."[14] The classical world certainly had a higher tolerance for didacticism than we do today, as evidenced by the popularity of the didactic writings of Hesiod, Virgil, Horace, and, indeed, Gregory himself. Scholars of Saint Ambrose of Milan have shown how his hymns were written to directly combat the faulty theology of the popular Arian sect, which had its own hymn writers.[15] Gregory mentions in "On the Metered" that he sees himself in competition with non-Christian poets:

> I write
> To win the current battle which we wage with words
> Where each side seeks, through books, linguistic victory.[16]

This is a battle not for literary prizes, but for popularity and cultural staying power. His victory in this regard depends on his ability to actually achieve poetic excellence. As Quasten writes, Gregory "wished first of all to prove that the new Christian culture was no longer inferior in any way to the pagan. Secondly, since certain heresies, especially that of Apollinaris, did not hesitate to spread their teachings in poetical garb, he finds it necessary to make use of the same weapon for successful refutation of their false doctrines."[17] Thus Gregory's "On the Genuine Books of the God-

---

12. Quasten, *Patrology*, 3:244.
13. Quasten, *Patrology*, 3:244.
14. Pope, *Rape of the Lock*, 12.
15. White, *Early Latin Christian Poets*, 47.
16. Gregory Nazianzus, "Eis Ta Emmetra," ll. 46–49.
17. Quasten, *Patrology*, 3:244.

Breathed Writings," should be read in light of these considerations. It is not Gregory's intention to pour out his heart, nor be strikingly original. It is his goal to say "what oft was thought" and taught by Christians "but ne'er so well expressed" by them. The poem is a true testing ground of Gregory's didactic poetics. The condescension of the Son of God and the salvation of the human race is so poetic a subject that even New Testament writers wander into verse to express it. But the listing of difficult-to-pronounce book titles in order to delineate genuine from non-genuine scripture texts is indeed toilsome, and can feel tedious, even bitter. It is precisely the canon debate that so dearly needs a little sweetening.

In conclusion, then, let us consider where and how in this poem Gregory succeeds according to his own poetics. Does Gregory's meter successfully mitigate the tedium of the subject? Much of this depends upon the success of the meter as meter. As already mentioned, Gregory does not—perhaps cannot—maintain the same meter over the course of poem. He switches between dactylic hexameter and iambic trimeter. I would like to delineate several types of successful lines in the poem: the first are those that are metrically perfect, and so shape their content as to create lines of beauty and balance. There are at least a dozen of these lines: certainly the first eight, and the handful of dactylic lines that punctuate the rest of the poem. Second are lines that adopt conventional variances, such as an extra short syllable to accommodate an author's name, or spondees in place of iambs. Many of the 20 or so iambic lines are like this, some more regular than others. Then there are lines of metrical irregularity that, while distinctly odd, have been balanced by Gregory such that there is a metrical beauty to them. Two lines in particular stand out in this regard:

> These tell eldest of things, things wise Hebrews believe . . .
> ....
> Chronicles afterward. Last, Ezra you must possess too.[18]

---

18. Gregory Nazianzus, "On the Genuine Books of the God-Breathed Writing," ll. 10, 15.

The Sweetened List

These are strange variants of dactylic hexameter that in Greek have a recognizable, if uncommon, pattern. They also bookend Gregory's presentation of the books of Old Testament History, a formal decision that smacks of poetic intention—an arrangement of that which is irregular into a higher, balanced structure. Still, the judicious reader must admit a handful of lines—I would count around six, though some subjectivity is involved in such judgments—that are metrically defective. But overall Gregory has succeeded in fitting the canon list into meter.

Gregory's list does, however, lack something that Athanasius's list possesses, and that is a discussion of what to do with deuterocanonical books. Athanasius, like Eusebius before him, speaks of "other books besides these not indeed included in the Canon, but appointed by the Fathers to be read by those who newly join us, and who wish for instruction in the word of godliness."[19] He goes on to list the Wisdom of Solomon, Esther, the Shepherd of Hermas, and a few others. These he distinguishes from truly heretical books, which he rejects entirely. In his poem Gregory does not give himself the chance or the space to discuss such nuances. This is not to say that such distinctions are impossible in verse, just that Gregory's chosen tone and structure do not allow for them. His only distinction is between the genuine and the alien, the *gneisiais* and the *xeineisi*. In "On the Metered" Gregory makes a similar distinction:

> Discard
> All words but those that God inspired and keep them close.
> Become, yourself, a harbor to hold back the storm.[20]

True to type, Gregory's rhetorical flair can at times hide nuance in shadow even as it illumines plain truth like lightning.

Gregory calls the writing of poetry a "discipline [of] soul," and through this discipline he seeks to write more sweetly, more winningly, of that which his soul loves, of that which he sees as of great importance for all humans. If his ambition sometimes

---

19. Athanasius, "Letter XXXIX," 552.
20. Gregory Nazianzus, "Eis Ta Emmetra," ll. 9–11.

outstrips his ability, his work is no less indelible. In Gregory, then, we see a Church Father who achieved what few before his generation had: he has taken his love for Christian doctrine and made it the impetus for high art. His contemporaries Ephrem the Syrian and Ambrose were doing the same, as would Augustine, soon. But among these, Gregory was one of the only Fathers to attempt a poem on the canon, a bitterly disputed matter made, through meter, more sweet.

4

A New Macrina

Toward a Cappadocian Poetics for the Twenty-First Century

When we speak of the fourth-century Cappadocians, we speak of three siblings—Macrina the Younger, Basil of Caesarea, and Gregory of Nyssa—along with their friend, Gregory of Nazianzus. Macrina, eldest of the siblings, acted as the moral compass and spiritual guide to her family. When Basil, who attended the famous Academy at Athens alongside Gregory of Nazianzus, came home full of secular ambitions, Macrina convinced him to instead dedicate his life to monasticism and Christian ministry. When Basil died, Macrina's philosophical consolation of her younger brother Gregory became the famous dialogue *On the Soul and Resurrection*. Finally, Basil's Macrina-inspired theology and work on behalf of the poor was praised by Gregory Nazianzus and informed his later theological orations and poems. While important work has been done on both the theological anthropology of the Cappadocians and on the poems of Gregory Nazianzus in particular, the ways in which Gregory's poetics is coherent and fruitfully interacts with the theological anthropology of his Cappadocian peers is relatively unexplored. A fleshed-out Cappadocian poetics has the opportunity to speak to key social and ethical concerns in modern critical theory, chief among them gender, class, and the role of aesthetic form in the creation of virtue within an individual and justice within communities.

CAPPADOCIAN THEOLOGICAL ANTHROPOLOGY

The thought of all four Cappadocians is grounded in a theological anthropology, that is, a theory of the nature of humans with reference to their divine origin and destiny. One of the earliest works in which we find the Cappadocian theological anthropology articulated is Basil's first discourse "On the Origin of Humanity." In this discourse, Basil discusses Gen 1:26: "Let us make the human being according to our image and likeness." Basil explains that the image of God in man is not physical, but intellectual: it is "the superiority of reason."[1] Basil clarifies that there are two "human beings, one the sense perceptible, and one hidden under the sense perceptible, invisible, the inner human. Therefore we have an inner human being, and we are somehow double, and it is truly said that we are that which is within."[2] Further, Basil distinguishes between the image and the likeness of God:

> In our initial structure co-originates and exists our coming into being according to the image of God. By free choice we are conformed to that which is according to the likeness of God.... He has made us with the power to become like God. And in giving us the power to become like God he let us be artisans of the likeness to God, so that the reward for the work would be ours.[3]

To drive home this final point, Basil provides a brief catechism: "How do we come to be according to the likeness? Through the Gospels. What is Christianity? Likeness to God as far as is possible for human nature."[4] Thus, for Basil, humans are created as beings

---

1. Basil the Great, *On the Human Condition*, 36.
2. Basil the Great, *On the Human Condition*, 36.
3. Basil the Great, *On the Human Condition*, 43–44.
4. Basil the Great, *On the Human Condition*, 45.

of special dignity, with rational souls intended to rule the physical body, and with free will in order to become like God through a Christian life grounded in the Gospels.

In Gregory of Nyssa's record of his dialogue with Macrina, likely written around 380, Macrina articulates a similar anthropology to Basil, but couches it in eschatological terms. "Human nature," she explains, "was a divine sort of thing, before humanity started on the course of evil."[5] But in the resurrection, "God intends to set before everyone the participation of the good things in Him, which the Scripture says eye has not seen, nor ear heard, nor thought attained. This is nothing else, according to my judgment, but to be in God Himself."[6] Such a blessed state of purification from evil and union with God is made possible because of the image of God in which humans are made: "When such things are cleansed and purified away by the treatment through fire, each of the better qualities will enter in their place: incorruptibility, life, honor, grace, glory, power, and whatever else of this kind we recognize in God himself and in His image, which is our human nature."[7] Neither Basil nor Macrina shies from the reality of human weakness and sin, but they see such a state as ultimately temporary and practically reversible: God has made humans to be like Him, has given them reason with which to rule themselves, and a free will with which to choose a life of God-likeness. The ultimate reward for this will be union with the divine source of all, God himself. And the path of god-likeness and ultimate union is learned through the New Testament Gospels.

SOCIO-POLITICAL IMPLICATIONS OF CAPPADOCIAN ANTHROPOLOGY

Cappadocian anthropology is *theandric*, that is, concerned with the union of God and humanity. The practical implications of

---

5. Gregory of Nyssa, *On the Soul and Resurrection*, 113.
6. Gregory of Nyssa, *On the Soul and Resurrection*, 115.
7. Gregory of Nyssa, *On the Soul and Resurrection*, 115.

theandric anthropology for the Cappadocians were wide ranging and radical. Slavery, for instance, was out of the question for Gregory of Nyssa, as Nonna Verna Harrison has recently discussed.[8] We will focus on two of these implications: gender and class. If all humans are essentially and by nature equal, the Cappadocians thought, then the division between male and female was not as fundamental as some might believe. Basil writes: "The woman also possesses creation according to the image of God, as indeed does the man. The natures are alike of equal honor, the virtues are equal, the struggles equal, the judgment alike. Let her not say 'I am weak.' The weakness is in the flesh, in the soul is power."[9] For Basil, the distinction between male and female is a distinction in body only, not in soul, and thus the same honor, dignity, and moral necessity can be ascribed to males and females equally. In his treatise "On the Making of Man," Gregory of Nyssa fundamentally agrees:

> While two natures—the Divine and incorporeal nature, and the irrational life of brutes—are separated from each other as extremes, human nature is the mean between them: for in the compound nature of man we may behold a part of each of the natures I have mentioned—of the Divine, the rational and intelligent element, which does not admit the distinction of male and female; of the irrational, our bodily form and structure, divided into male and female: for each of these elements is certainly to be found in all that partakes of human life. That the intellectual element, however, precedes the other, we learn as from one who gives in order an account of the making of man; and we learn also that his community and kindred with the irrational is for man a provision for reproduction. For he says first that God created man in the image of God (showing by these words, as the Apostle says, that in such a being there is no male or female): then he adds the peculiar attributes of human nature, "male and female created He them."[10]

---

8. See Harrison, *God's Many-Splendored Image*, 97–99.
9. Basil the Great, *On the Human Condition*, 46.
10. Gregory of Nyssa, *On the Making of Man*, 16.9.

A New Macrina

Gregory agrees with his older brother that there is a "Divine, rational and intelligent" element in all humans, which was created before the division into sexes, and in which the nature of humans resides. While acknowledging that the division of human bodies into sexes is necessary for biological reproduction, like Basil before him, Gregory sees this distinction as making little difference to the origin, nature, and calling of all humans.

Basil does, at times, allow himself to admit that there may be a practical, moral distinction between males and females: "When has the nature of man been able to match the nature of woman in patiently passing through her own life? When has man been able to imitate the vigor of women in fastings, the love of toil in prayers, the abundance in tears, the readiness for good works?"[11] It is indicative of Basil's monastic focus that his gentle ribbing of men for not measuring up to women has little to do with the traditional gender stereotypes of female domesticity or male headship. Basil's playing field is ascetic endeavor, an endeavor he sees as the calling of both men and women, and in this he finds men wanting and women exemplary.

Gregory's biography of his sister is a prime example of the Cappadocian image of exemplary womanhood. Gregory starts his *Life of Macrina* by praising his sister as one "who so surpassed her sex . . . a woman who raised herself by 'philosophy' to the greatest height of human virtue."[12] If we read Gregory's description of Macrina "surpassing her sex" in light of both his own and Basil's anthropology, we can see "sex" as meaning not some inherently flawed nature, but instead the expectations that fourth-century society placed upon those with female bodies. Further, Gregory's description of Macrina as philosopher is fully in line with his description, in *On the Making of Man*, of women possessing a "Divine, rational and intelligent element." Again and again throughout *The Life of Macrina*, we see Macrina acting as a unique kind of philosopher. Her education avoids pagan literature, and instead "such parts of inspired Scripture as you would think were incomprehensible to

---

11. Basil the Great, *On the Human Condition*, 46.
12. Gregory of Nyssa, *Life of Macrina*, 18–19.

young children were the subject of the girl's studies; in particular the Wisdom of Solomon, and those parts of it especially which have an ethical bearing. Nor was she ignorant of any part of the Psalter, but at stated times she recited every part of it."[13] Macrina uses her knowledge to instruct her brothers, especially Basil:

> He was puffed up beyond measure with the pride of oratory and looked down on the local dignitaries, excelling in his own estimation all the men of learning and position. Nevertheless Macrina took him in hand, and with such speed did she draw him also toward the mark of philosophy that he forsook the glories of this world and despised fame gained by speaking, and deserted it for this busy life where one toils with one's hands.[14]

Having attended the Academy at Athens, Basil was one of the best educated men in his world. But Macrina supersedes all secular education with her philosophy.

When Gregory of Nyssa is in deep mourning over Basil's death and his sister's sickness, Macrina again acts as teacher:

> When in the course of conversation mention was made of the great Basil, my soul was saddened and my face fell dejectedly. But so far was she from sharing in my affliction that, treating the mention of the saint as an occasion for yet loftier philosophy, she discussed various subjects, inquiring into human affairs and revealing in her conversation the divine purpose concealed in disasters. Besides this, she discussed the future life, as if inspired by the Holy Spirit, so that it almost seemed as if my soul were lifted by the help of her words away from mortal nature and placed within the heavenly sanctuary.[15]

Gregory's *On the Soul and Resurrection* is his detailed account of this "loftier philosophy" of Macrina. Given that Macrina quotes Plato frequently in Gregory's dialogue, it is clear that in his final writings about her, Gregory wants his readers to see Macrina as

13. Gregory of Nyssa, *Life of Macrina*, 22.
14. Gregory of Nyssa, *Life of Macrina*, 27–28.
15. Gregory of Nyssa, *Life of Macrina*, 45.

A New Macrina

a new Socrates, comforting and uplifting her disciples in the face of death, just as Socrates did in Plato's dialogue *Phaedo*. But for Gregory, Macrina is a new and better Socrates. For one thing, she is a woman, and for another she is a Christian, and can add to the wisdom of the pagans the God-inspired wisdom of the scriptures and the god-like life of monastic ascesis. In fact, other than philosopher, Gregory's favorite image of Macrina is as athlete:

> When her noble character had been tested by these different accessions of trouble, in every respect the metal of her soul was proved to be unadulterated and undefiled. The first test was the loss of the one brother, the second the parting from her mother, the third was when the common glory of the family, great Basil, was removed from human life. So she remained, like an invincible athlete in no wise broken by the assault of troubles.[16]

According to Gregory, Macrina was quite beautiful and inspired competition among the rich bachelors in her town. But tragedy and ingenuity let Macrina escape marriage. First, the man who her father picked for her to marry died suddenly while they were still engaged. Macrina cleverly claimed that she would honor his memory as if she had married him, and could thus never marry another, lest she commit adultery. Free from the social expectations of marriage, which seem to have been uninteresting to her, Macrina set about on a work that truly mattered to her: the transformation of her community along egalitarian lines.

Macrina's egalitarian project in Cappadocia brings us to the other major implication of the Cappadocian theological anthropology: the dissolution of class distinctions and the just distribution of wealth. Macrina began her transformation of her society with her household:

> Now that all the distractions of the material life had been removed, Macrina persuaded her mother to give up her ordinary life and all showy style of living and the services of domestics to point of view down to that of the masses, and to share the life of the maids, treating all her slave

16. Gregory of Nyssa, *Life of Macrina*, 40–41.

girls and menials as if they were sisters and belonged to the same rank as herself.¹⁷

Thus, because of Macrina the wealth of Macrina's family became dispersed throughout her community instead of being passed on from generation to aristocratic generation within her family. Indeed, after being taught by Macrina, Basil embraces "the renunciation of property . . . lest anything should impede the life of virtue."¹⁸ Basil would have been giving up quite an inheritance, an inheritance that would have secured his place as a prominent landholder in Cappadocia. Instead, Basil, Macrina, and their mother Emmelia all became monastics, and the cycle of aristocratic inheritance was dismantled. It must be recognized that the motivation for such a shift in class and economics is not primarily driven by some materialist theory of labor, but by an explicitly theological-ascetic philosophy of the ethical life.

In his sermons on wealth and poverty, Basil drove home a similar principle: that wealth was given to aristocrats not to hoard, but to share, even to the point of equal distribution of wealth within the community.

> When all share alike, disbursing their possessions among themselves, they each receive a small portion for their individual needs. Thus, those who love their neighbor as themselves possess nothing more than their neighbor; yet surely you seem to have great possessions! How else can this be, but that you have preferred your own enjoyment to the consolation of many. For the more you abound in wealth, the more you lack in love.¹⁹

Basil's friend Gregory Nazianzus also preached this sort of radical economics. As John McGuckin explains:

> For Gregory almsgiving was far more than the effete notion of occasional donations to the needy which the word suggests today . . . in Gregory's thought, the care of the

---

17. Gregory of Nyssa, *Life of Macrina*, 28–29.
18. Gregory of Nyssa, *Life of Macrina*, 28.
19. Basil the Great, *On Social Justice*, 43.

poor is a privilege laid upon Christians which serves to conform them to the Deity, a major element in his favorite conception of the Christ-life which he designated as *Theosis*—the transfiguration into the divine life, of which celibacy, the personal asceticism of a simplified lifestyle, and above all scholarly seclusion (the formation for the human *Nous*), both formed essential parts.[20]

Though McGuckin is here describing Gregory's thought, he could equally be describing the almsgiving, celibate, ascetic, and scholarly Macrina, a model not just of womanhood, but of true human potential for all the Cappadocians: the potential for what Gregory calls *theosis* and Basil calls "god-likeness."

CAPPADOCIAN POETICS

The austere and at times radical nature of Cappadocian thought may seem to leave little time for artistic or literary pursuits. But we have already seen that Macrina and Gregory Nazianzus were dedicated scholars. Gregory of Nyssa points out that Macrina was especially knowledgeable about the Psalms—the greatest trove of poetry in the Hebrew scriptures. And though Macrina shunned the pagan classics, Basil saw them as useful for training in virtue. In his "Address to Young Men on the Right Use of Greek Literature," he explains:

> We must be conversant with poets, with historians, with orators, indeed with all men who may further our soul's salvation. Just as dyers prepare the cloth before they apply the dye, be it purple or any other color, so indeed must we also, if we would preserve indelible the idea of the true virtue, become first initiated in the pagan lore, then at length give special heed to the sacred and divine teachings, even as we first accustom ourselves to the sun's reflection in the water, and then become able to turn our eyes upon the very sun itself.[21]

20. McGuckin, *Saint Gregory of Nazianzus*, 12–13.
21. Basil the Great, *Essays on the Study and Use of Poetry*, 103.

Basil's "Address" along with Macrina's favored texts are important elements in the Cappadocian attitude toward literature, but they do not form a complete poetics. Most importantly, they do not take into account the nature of literary creation, nor its place, if any, in the larger theandric anthropology. It would remain up to Gregory of Nazianzus to articulate this.

In the final decade of his life, Gregory turned to poetry. Though it is difficult to date his poems exactly, most agree that they were written between his retirement in 381 and his death around 390. One of the most important poems written during this period, as we have seen in earlier chapters, was *Eis Ta Emmetra*, or "On the Metered." This 103-line poem is central to a Cappadocian understanding of literary art. Gregory begins his poem with a complaint:

> I see the many penning—in this life of ours—
> A language that's unmetered; they just let it flow
> And so erase each faded hour with such strained work
> According none a blessing—it's all glottal waste.[22]

Gregory's complaint is against those who write without regard to poetic form. The poetic form he has in mind is the quantitative verse of late antique Greek, which was based on repeating patterns of long and short syllables. To write in an unmetered fashion is to create waste, and not poetry at all. He calls such unmetered writing "only fit for tyrants' pens,"[23] and recommends that his readers

> discard
> All words but those that God inspired and keep them close;
> Become, yourself, a harbor to hold back the storm.[24]

So far, Gregory sounds like Macrina, avoiding useless texts and holding only to scripture. But Gregory is up to something more. He does not pick moral vice to condemn in literature, but rather

---

22. Gregory Nazianzus, "Eis Ta Emmetra," ll. 1–4.
23. Gregory Nazianzus, "Eis Ta Emmetra," l. 5.
24. Gregory Nazianzus, "Eis Ta Emmetra," ll. 9–11.

formal disorder. And he chooses to write about it in a highly formal poem with lines of iambic hexameter.

After answering those who accuse him of desire for fame, Gregory presents his famous four reasons why he writes poetry. In doing so Gregory develops a detailed explanation of how poetry is involved in individual moral development, in pedagogy, in culture, and in light of eternity. First, Gregory presents an ascetic reason for writing poetry:

> With measured labor—first—I discipline my soul,
> For writing lines can order my unmetered mind,
> And keep my greedy pen in check—instead I spend
> My sweat on metric form.[25]

Just as he condemns those who ignore form in their writing, Gregory holds himself to a standard of "measured labor" and "metric form." This does not just result in well-structured poetry, but works against his "unmetered mind" and his desire to write too much. Poetry, then, is first an ascetic discipline, akin to the list McGuckin provides above: "almsgiving... celibacy... a simplified lifestyle... scholarly seclusion."[26]

Building upon a foundation of ascesis, Gregory adds his second reason for writing:

> Second, I write for youths,
> And for whoever takes a deep delight in words—
> My verses read like sugar with elixir mixed,
> They can win men to virtue's work and discipline,
> By sweetening with art the bitterness of law.[27]

Not only is poetry a practice that can instill discipline in the writer—it can instill virtue and discipline in the reader. It does this by "sweetening with art" those subjects that on their own might seem bitter. As we have seen earlier, Gregory adds Platonic depth to what might otherwise seem shallow:

---

25. Gregory Nazianzus, "Eis Ta Emmetra," ll. 33–37.
26. McGuckin, *Saint Gregory of Nazianzus*, 12–13.
27. Gregory Nazianzus, "Eis Ta Emmetra," ll. 37–41.

The Poets and the Fathers

> I
> Have written hymns and plays for those who wish to play,
> But not be hindered in their quest for Beauty.[28]

Gregory takes as given two things about humans: they wish to playfully delight in art and culture, while at the same time pursuing their ultimate end, the transcendental beauty that is the Divine source of all things. While the unmetered tyrannical verse that he condemns in his opening lines might hinder its audience from their ultimate quest, Gregory's verse, ordered and virtue-praising as it is, will facilitate both the temporary delights of art in living culture, and the greater quest beyond it.

Gregory's third reason is one he seems almost ashamed of:

> Third—
> And if this just sounds petty let me know—I write
> To win the current battle which we wage with words;
> Where each side seeks, through books, linguistic victory.[29]

Though in his preface to the four reasons, Gregory claimed he does not seek "a glory wholly hollow,"[30] here he admits that he does seek a sort of literary victory. Such victory is complicated, but surely involves some sort of popular acclaim, or at least popular persuasion. Growing up in the Constantinian era in which he did, Gregory was used to something that was relatively new to Christians: a legal right to openly speak and write about their beliefs in a pluralistic public square where no one sect, philosophical or religious, was established by the government. Because the sword of the government would not be wielded on behalf of anyone's beliefs, all were left to the power of the pen and the orator's pulpit as their weapons of persuasion.

Gregory is cognizant of the dangers of seeking earthly success as one's primary end, and so in the midst of his third reason he reminds his readers of their ultimate ends:

---

28. Gregory Nazianzus, "Eis Ta Emmetra," ll. 44–46.
29. Gregory Nazianzus, "Eis Ta Emmetra," ll. 46–48.
30. Gregory Nazianzus, "Eis Ta Emmetra," l. 27.

(I speak of language that partakes in beauty, though
The highest Beauty is through contemplation reached.)[31]

This "Beauty," in Greek *kalos*, is the same Beauty that he refers to in his second reason. Again and again, Gregory seeks to tie his poetics to the larger context of theandric anthropology, and in doing so, he lends this anthropology an aesthetic nuance: instead of God, the Good, or the One, he characterizes the Divine Nature as "Beauty."

In his fourth and final reason, Gregory places before his readers the reality of death:

> And fourth, when winter wind brings sickness, struggle, death,
> My poems comfort me, swan-like old man; they lull
> Me with their wings, embolden me like woodwind hymns—
> No threnodies, but songs to lead me ever on.

Just as poetry can provide temporary delights to those looking for popular entertainment, it can also provide temporary balm to those who are suffering. "Poems comfort . . . lull," and, finally, "embolden" the human in the face of death. Because the ultimate goal of human life is to be made like God, to be united with the Beauty in which all beautiful language partakes, sickness and death are a passageway, not an end, and poetry at its best can "lead [one] ever on" through death into eternity. This is, in part, because a poem that truly partakes in beauty is indeed already giving one a foretaste of union with the Beauty that is God. When we read this principle back into Gregory's second, "spoonful of sugar" reason, the sugar begins to look not so saccharine: it is sweet because true Beauty is infused within it. And this participation in beauty is made possible through the sweat and work of shaping each line according to rigorous form.

To sum up, we must reiterate that a Cappadocian poetics first concerns itself with the individual creator, demanding of them the rigorous, soul-disciplining work of formally ordering language. Second, a Cappadocian poetics concerns itself with

---

31. Gregory Nazianzus, "Eis Ta Emmetra," ll. 49–50.

the educational needs of the poet's community of readers. They need to be persuaded to follow virtue, but they also, by nature, love delight and beauty. Poetry, if properly crafted, can provide both. Third, a Cappadocian poetics concerns itself with the larger culture beyond the poet's immediate community: a whole, pluralistic culture, abounding with sophistry, in which well-metered, virtue-praising poetry can gain prominence among the scrum of striving literatures. Finally, a Cappadocian poetics returns to the individual, and recognizes a role for poetry in the suffering, sickness, and death that are natural to the human's mortal state. In all of these realms of concern, Cappadocian poetics recognizes the ultimate end of human life is not to conform to any temporary, cultural glory or identity, but rather to seek one's end in Divine-human communion, a communion wherein transcendent Beauty is found.

As I have tried to suggest in my description of Gregory's Cappadocian poetics, his reasons for writing are wholly compatible with the anthropological and socio-political goals of Macrina, Basil, and Gregory of Nyssa. Unfortunately, Gregory's second reason can sometimes give readers pause, tending, as it can, toward a simple moralism if removed from the Cappadocian context. When writers, especially Christian writers, have spoken of using art to teach morals, the resulting art has often been poorly made and the morals simplistic. If Gregory's poetics produced a literature that was used to simply make young Christians follow the rules and be polite, it would be unimpressive at best and complicit in injustice at worst. For the Cappadocian outlook is one of social change; it calls for the disruption of aristocratic greed and for insubordination to gender norms when the cause of justice and faithfulness to God may be served thereby. Thus, when Gregory Nazianzus speaks of virtue and law in his poetics, I think it best to see to see the ethical ideals of Gregory's poetics as embodied in Macrina, and the goal of each poem as the creation, whenever possible, of a new Macrina in each reader.

A New Macrina

CAPPADOCIAN POETICS AND LITERARY THEORY

I would like to suggest how the Cappadocian poetics I have attempted to articulate could be put into conversation with two major strands in recent literary theory. First, since I have employed the term *insubordination*, I have brought the thought of Judith Butler into the conversation. Butler, as the apostle of Derrida's deconstruction, would likely be bewildered by the Cappadocians' strong belief in things like essences, natures, and transcendent deities. Butler writes:

> There is no volitional subject behind the mime who decides, as it were, which gender it will be today. On the contrary, the very possibility of becoming a viable subject requires that a certain gender mime be already underway. The being of the subject is no more self-identical than the being of any gender; in fact, coherent gender, achieved through an apparent repetition of the same, produces as its effect the illusion of a prior and volitional subject.[32]

Macrina, Basil, and the Gregorys would all strongly assert, contra Butler, that each human is a rational, volitional subject, and that such a subject is beyond both gender-performance and sexuality. For them, the human soul is non-sexed because it is non-physical. But at the physical, practical level, the Cappadocians share with Butler a championing of the individual freedom to disregard the performative behaviors that a culture presents as compulsory for a given gender or sex, especially when such prescribed performances are unjust. In Butler's view, gender "is a compulsory performance in the sense that acting out of line with heterosexual norms brings with it ostracism, punishment, and violence, not to mention the transgressive pleasures produced by those very prohibitions."[33] Macrina's individual rejection of matrimony, and her larger community's turning away from aristocratic domesticity toward ascesis and monasticism is an example of such insubordination to expected roles for women. But whereas Butler's metaphysics tends

---

32. Butler, "Imitation and Gender Insubordination," 957.
33. Butler, "Imitation and Gender Insubordination," 957–58.

toward a skepticism of any transcendent meaning or immortal subject, Macrina's metaphysics is downright mystical: it is because all humans possess an essentially non-sexed rational soul and are made for union with a metaphysical Deity that all earthy roles for the sexes are temporary, imperfect things that the Christian is free to reject if they prove to be obstacles to Christian faithfulness.[34]

The political nature of these matters makes a Cappadocian poetics a good conversation partner for the ethical theory of Martha Nussbaum as well. In her 1997 *Cultivating Humanity*, Nussbaum argues that literature can and should "play a vital role in educating citizens of the world," and that one should develop, through literary education, "an informed and compassionate vision of the different."[35] Nussbaum argues that those who claim "it is inappropriate to approach literature with a 'political agenda'" have embraced "an extreme kind of aesthetic formalism that is sterile and unappealing."[36] While the Cappadocians have a decidedly socio-political focus, they also embrace a strong formalism. But this formalism is not sterile; it is explicitly ethical, the ascetic basis for a poetics that embraces and seeks ethical education and change within the individual soul, the immediate community, and the larger culture of the poet. While post-Romantic aesthetics often associates formalism with sterility and indifference to communal and political matters, the Cappadocians hold to the older, Platonic association between the justly ordered soul and the justly ordered society. A Cappadocian poetics, then, can make common cause with the political concerns of both gender and ethical approaches to poetics, but can balance their respective tendencies toward metaphysical skepticism and anti-formalism through a grounding in an ascetic understanding of form and theandric anthropology.

---

34. That there are moral parameters to sexual behavior is a presupposition for the Cappadocians, given that in their view any insubordination to cultural conceptions of gender is always motivated by radical acts of Christian ascesis and social-justice-making. Insubordination of gender roles or sexual mores for the sake of mere bodily gratification would have been condemned by the Cappadocians as morally reprehensible.

35. Nussbaum, "Cultivating Humanity," 385.

36. Nussbaum, "Cultivating Humanity," 385.

5

The Virtue of Silence
Ethics and Quietude in the Poems of Henry Wadsworth Longfellow

> We will be patient, and assuage the feeling
>   We may not wholly stay;
> By silence sanctifying, not concealing
>   The grief that must have its way.[1]

THE ABOVE LINES WERE written by the American poet Henry Wadsworth Longfellow in 1849, referring, in part, to his own grief at the recent loss of his daughter. According to Longfellow, silence need not merely conceal grief; it can sanctify it. In this essay I mean to discuss the ethics of silence—the power of silence to sanctify, and of the power of silence to conceal. I realize there is an irony in the choice of silence as a topic for an essay's worth of words. But we could say that poetry—in its ascetic adherence to rules of metrics, its linguistic condensation, its wide, white margins, and its relative brevity when compared with other genres of literature—is the closest that literary endeavor can come to silence. Thus, it is to poetry I turn, in particular those poems in which Longfellow discusses the relationship between silence and the life of virtue. I

---

1. Longfellow, *Complete Poetical Works*, 134.

trace the development of the concept of silence from Longfellow's early masterpiece *Evangeline*, in which we find the beginnings of a theological ethics of silence, through to the late sonnet "The Three Silences of Molinos," where the poet presents a more detailed and nuanced picture of the sanctifying power of silence. And we will end with a nod toward Longfellow's posthumously published *Michael Angelo: A Fragment*, in which we are warned against a kind of silence that conceals virtue.

Longfellow began his literary career in the 1830s and '40s as a highly didactic, if not always explicitly religious, poet. This fit the convention of the time. Ben Franklin's *Poor Richard* rhymes were still ringing in the New England air when Longfellow joined in, calling his readers to be:

> up and doing,
> With a heart for any fate;
> Still achieving, still pursuing,
> Learn to labor and to wait.[2]

Such didacticism earned Longfellow a few critics, among them Edgar Allen Poe, but many more fans. However, Longfellow's academic interests did not lay in simple didactics, but rather in the literature and traditions of the Old World. He was a dutiful student of the literature of the European continent. He explored not just poetry, but theological writings as well—the Church Fathers, Dante, and the Spanish mystics all crowded the bookshelves of his early career. Sadly, the influence that these writers exerted upon Longfellow's poems remains largely unexplored.

The first major indication that Longfellow had more to offer than didactic lyrics was the publication of *Evangeline*, the poet's first long narrative poem, in 1847. *Evangeline* tells the story of two French Canadian lovers—Evangeline and Gabriel—who are separated the day before their wedding and sent into exile. Evangeline vows to search for Gabriel and, encouraged by her priest, ranges across pre-revolution America in her quasi-epic quest. Whereas Longfellow's shorter poetic narratives up until this point had been

---

2. Longfellow, *Complete Poetical Works*, 4.

straightforward and largely unencumbered by doctrinal complexities, in *Evangeline* the character of the priest, Father Felician, acts as the theological interpreter of Evangeline's journey. In a sermon he gives at the center of the poem, he tells Evangeline that her desire to seek for Gabriel will have great spiritual merit:

> Patience, accomplish thy labor, accomplish thy work of affection,
> Sorrow and silence are strong, and patient endurance is godlike.
> Therefore accomplish thy labor of love till the heart is made godlike,
> Purified, strengthened, perfected, and rendered more worthy of heaven.[3]

Nestled within this call to achieve godlikeness through ethical and ascetic activity is the concept of silence. "Sorrow and silence," we learn, are strong, and in the last two lines of the passage Felician explains that godlikeness is state of purity, strength, perfection, and worthiness of Heaven. Thus silence contributes to strength, which contributes to godlikeness. In contemporary theological language, we would call Felician's theology here one of ethical deification, wherein the human who acquires ethical, divine attributes may be called godlike.[4] And silence is one of these attributes that can render the human godlike.

Longfellow did not make this up, of course. He found it, among other places, in his research in Patristics, conducted in the early 1830s. In a lecture on the Church Fathers that Longfellow presented to his classes in 1832, he uses a commentary by the Lutheran theologian Johann Mosheim on the theology of Origen. In Mosheim's explanation of the mystic theology of Origen and his followers, he writes: "they maintained that silence, tranquility, repose, and solitude, accompanied with such acts of mortification as might tend to extenuate and exhaust the body, were the means by which the hidden and internal word was excited to produce

---

3. Longfellow, *Complete Poetical Works*, 105.

4. For a long discussion of deification language in Longfellow, see Bartel, *Glimpses of Her Father's Glory*.

its latent virtues, and to instruct men in the knowledge of divine things."⁵ Mosheim explains that when silence, along with the other ascetic acts, is pursued, the Christian at last achieves a "happy union" with God himself.⁶

Though theological research lies behind Longfellow's inclusion of silence as an ethical activity which contributes to godlikeness, there is little highlighting or dramatizing of the practice of silence in the text of *Evangeline*. Instead Longfellow focuses on the other attributes Felician mentions: suffering, patient endurance, and affectionate love. Thus, though we find the beginnings of a theological ethics of silence in *Evangeline*, it remains underdeveloped, illustrated by no dramatic examples in the plot. Further, silence here seems single and simple—it does not admit of subcategories.

SILENCE AND MOLINOS

Evangeline marked the advent of Longfellow the narrative poet, and it is largely on his narrative poems that Longfellow's reputation now rests: *Evangeline, The Song of Hiawatha, The Courtship of Miles Standish, The Tales from a Wayside Inn*, and his crowning academic achievement, the first complete American translation of Dante's *Divine Comedy*. But as he composed his long, mature narratives, he also honed his craft as a sonneteer. And surprisingly, even when his narrative works have been out of critical favor, Longfellow's sonnets have continued to be considered among the best in American literature.

It is in one of these sonnets, "The Three Silences of Molinos," that Longfellow returns to and builds upon the ethics of quietude that he began in *Evangeline*. But rather than the doctrine of the Church Fathers, it is the doctrines of Spanish mysticism that directly influenced the "Three Silences" sonnet. The sonnet is an occasional one—Edward Wagenknecht has called it one of

---

5. Mosheim, *Ecclesiastical History*, 215.
6. Mosheim, *Ecclesiastical History*, 216.

Longfellow's only successful occasional poems.[7] Longfellow records in his diary for December 17, 1877, that he read the poem at "The 'Atlantic Dinner' at the Brunswick Hotel, to celebrate the thirtieth anniversary of the Magazine, and Whittier's seventieth birthday."[8] John Greenleaf Whittier was a lifelong friend of Longfellow, and though they sometimes differed over politics, Longfellow's sonnet pays the man considerable tribute:

> Three Silences there are: the first of speech,
>   The second of desire, the third of thought;
>   This is the lore a Spanish monk, distraught
>   With dreams and visions, was the first to teach.
> These Silences, commingling each with each,
>   Made up the perfect Silence, that he sought
>   And prayed for, and wherein at times he caught
>   Mysterious sounds from realms beyond our reach.
> O thou, whose daily life anticipates
>   The life to come, and in whose thought and word
>   The spiritual world preponderates,
>
> Hermit of Amesbury! thou too hast heard
>   Voices and melodies from beyond the gates,
>   And speakest only when thy soul is stirred![9]

The Molinos that the title of the sonnet refers to is Miguel de Molinos, a seventeenth-century Spanish theologian whose popular book *The Spiritual Guide* was condemned by the Spanish Inquisition. Despite this condemnation, it is seen as the beginning of the Quietist movement within the church. A key element in Molinos's quietist theology is the use of silence to approach and unite with God. In chapter 16 of the *Spiritual Guide*, which acts as the conclusion of part 1 of the book, Molinos writes:

> There are three kinds of silence; the first of words, the second of desires, and the third of thoughts. The first is perfect; the second more perfect; and the third most perfect. In the first, that is, of words, virtue is acquired;

---

7. Wagenknecht, *Longfellow*, 78.
8. Longfellow, *Final Memorials*, 268.
9. Longfellow, *Complete Poetical Works*, 414.

in the second, to wit, of desires, quietness is attained to; in the third, of thoughts, internal recollection is gained. By not speaking, nor desiring, nor thinking, one arrives at the true and perfect mystical silence, wherein God speaks with the soul, communicates Himself to it, and in the abyss of its own depth teaches it the most perfect and exalted wisdom.[10]

Molinos goes on to explain that the conventional practice of silence, this is, the mere cessation of speech, is not enough to achieve mystical silence: "thou [must] wean thyself from all desires and thoughts. Rest in this mystical silence, and open the door, that so God may communicate Himself unto thee, unite with thee, and then form thee into Himself."[11] Here Molinos goes beyond his initial claim that in mystical silence God "speaks with the soul," writing that God will unite the silent soul with himself, and form it into himself. Here we find again—as in *Evangeline* and Mosheim's explanation of Origen's theology—the language of deification. And sure enough, Molinos then gives the example of the mystic Gregory Lopez as one who has achieved true silence, calling him a "Deified Man."[12]

Thus the "Three Silences" sonnet shares with *Evangeline* the quality of being inspired by theological sources that portray silence as a sanctifying, ethical activity that leads to deification. But there the similarities end. In the sonnet, silence is particularized, according to Molinos's categories, into three activities—silence of speech, silence of desire, and silence of thought—that all make up one "perfect" activity. Further, whereas *Evangeline*'s Father Felician links silence to strength and strength to godlikeness, in the eighth line of the sonnet Longfellow writes that Molinos, through silence, discerned "mysterious sounds from realms beyond our reach." This is a more modest fruit of silence than *Evangeline*'s godlikeness, and a step back from Molinos's own description of uniting with and being formed into God Himself.

10. Molinos, *Spiritual Guide*, 59.
11. Molinos, *Spiritual Guide*, 60.
12. Molinos, *Spiritual Guide*, 62.

The Virtue of Silence

Longfellow does not seem to be as interested in giving a full account of Molinos's theological ethics of silence as he is in presenting those elements of Molinos's doctrine that parallel the qualities of Whittier, to whom the poem is dedicated. In the sestet of the poem, we learn that Whittier, whom Longfellow calls the "hermit of Amesbury," has, like Molinos, "heard / Voices and melodies from beyond the gates." And Whittier's reputation as a prophetic writer—especially in his writings against slavery—gives Longfellow some precedent for treating Whittier as someone whose inspiration comes from heavenly realms.

Whittier himself at the end of his life wrote, "For many years I have not been able to read or write for more than half an hour at a time; often not so long."[13] Whittier attributes this disposition toward silence of words and thoughts not to spiritual practice, but to a "sensitive, nervous temperament."[14] Longfellow seems, then, to be taking some imaginative license with Whittier's disposition, implying that his "speaking only when stirred" is due to a quest for "the Perfect silence" of Molinos. In this Longfellow is not unlike his character Father Felician, interpreting a common human activity in spiritual terms, sanctifying it through the theological imagination.

Further evidence of Longfellow's theological mind is found when we compare the structures of the sonnet's octave and sestet with the first and last paragraphs of Molinos's chapter 16. In both Longfellow's octave and Molinos's first paragraph, the three types of silence are delineated, and the resulting divine communications are described. In Longfellow's sestet and Molinos's last two paragraphs we are presented with a historical example of a man who has sought and achieved true silence, and has begun to experience the fruits of such an endeavor.

---

13. Whittier, *Letters*, 454.
14. Whittier, *Letters*, 454.

SILENCE IN *MICHAEL ANGELO*

If in *Evangeline* and the "Three Silences" sonnet Longfellow develops the concept of a silence that sanctifies, in his last work he begins to sketch the concept of a silence that conceals. In his posthumously published dramatic fragment *Michael Angelo*, Longfellow introduces us to the young Italian socialite Julia, who is torn between the Florentine life of cultured ease and the ascetic life of the Christian mystic, which is represented by her friend and would-be tutor, Valdesso. When Julia finally asks Valdesso to "teach her" how to "harmonise the discord of her life," she includes a caveat:

> Point out to me the way of perfection
> And I will follow you; for you have made
> My soul enamored with it, and I cannot
> Rest satisfied until I find it out.
> But lead me privately, so that the world
> Hear not my steps; I would not give occasion
> For talk among the people.[15]

Valdesso sees through her request, and chides her:

> You would be free
> From the vexatious thoughts that come and go
> Through your imagination....
> You would attain divine perfection,
> And yet not turn your back upon the world;
> You would possess humility within
> But not reveal it in your outward actions;
> ....
> Would seem angelic in the sight of God
> Yet not too saint-like in the eyes of men;
> In short, would lead a holy Christian life
> In such a way that even your nearest friend
> Would not detect therein one circumstance
> To show a change from what it was before.[16]

---

15. Longfellow, *Complete Poetical Works*, 724.
16. Longfellow, *Complete Poetical Works*, 725.

In response, Julia confirms that Valdesso has "drawn / the portrait of [her] inner self as truly / as the most skillful painter."[17] In his exhortation, Valdesso describes a sort of silence—that of hiding one's journey toward virtue from one's community, so that no one can "hear" or "detect" one's ethical endeavors. I would like to call this the silence of concealment, which is different, and perhaps mutually exclusive, from the silence of sanctification that Longfellow describes in *Evangeline* and "The Three Silences of Molinos."

Lest we misunderstand the concealment of virtue that Julia asks for as humility, Valdesso explains that she does not even wish to "reveal [humility] in her outward actions." Using the examples of Evangeline and Whittier, Longfellow characterizes the one who practices sanctifying silence as someone whose attainment of perfection is apparent. Evangeline shines with "celestial light" from time to time throughout her journey, blessing, in this dramatic way, the people she meets. Likewise, Whittier "speaketh . . . when his soul is stirred," inspiring a whole nation with his divine words. Thus, according to Longfellow, the one who practices the silence of sanctification is not wholly silent about it. Their attainment of virtue will be somehow apparent. It is only the silence of concealment that renders virtue insensible.

While there is critical consensus that Longfellow's is a poetry largely concerned with ethics, the evidence that Longfellow's ethics are grounded in mystical Christian theology is almost wholly unexplored. Only father Richard Hickey, in his 1921 book *The Catholic Influence on Longfellow*, has acknowledged the great theological debt Longfellow owes not just to Dante, but to Molinos, Teresa of Avila, and other mystics of the Catholic tradition. And if Longfellow's debt to Catholic mysticism is underexplored, his grounding in patristics is almost wholly unacknowledged.[18] Instead, it has been the convention to describe Longfellow as theologically lax, uninterested in Christian doctrine, a man of practical ethics alone. I hope that this brief exploration of the theological ethics of silence

---

17. Longfellow, *Complete Poetical Works*, 725.

18. I have sought, for my part, to remedy this lack in my two previous volumes, *Glimpses of Her Father's Glory* and *The Heroines of Henry Longfellow*.

in Longfellow's poems can offer the beginnings of a change in our view of Longfellow and his importance in the tradition of American poets that have something to say not just about how to be good in this life, but about how to live a life that seeks likeness to and union with God at its end—of which silence, it seems, may be an important part.

6

From "The Soul" to "The Warning"
Longfellow, Education, and Abolition

HENRY WADSWORTH LONGFELLOW HAS not been primarily known as a theorist of education, nor as a political poet. His poetic imagination was most often taken with subjects long ago and far away from his context of nineteenth-century New England. When he did write about New England, it was mostly in pastoral lyrics, or narratives of the colonial or revolutionary past, as in *The Courtship of Miles Standish* and "Paul Revere's Ride." And yet, scholars have begun to see that these poems hint at the concerns of Longfellow's present day even as they explicitly occupy themselves with the past. For instance, Jill Lepore's 2011 article "How Longfellow Woke the Dead" highlights the ways in which the ostensibly revolution-focused poem "Paul Revere's Ride" hints at the horrors of slavery and the need for political action to end slavery.[1] Still, one need not look only to the subtext of Longfellow's poetry for contemporary political subjects, for Longfellow did write one volume of poetry in 1842 that explicitly focused on the present political concern of slavery. This was *Poems on Slavery*, which proved to be the most controversial of Longfellow's collections. To contemporaries like Nathaniel Hawthorne, Longfellow's choice of slavery as a subject

---

1. See Lepore, "How Longfellow Woke the Dead," 2–15.

seemed to come out of the blue. But the theoretical foundations of Longfellow's abolitionism had been discernible in his poetry since the late 1820s; indeed the final—and arguably best—poem in *Poems on Slavery* was a revision of a poem that Longfellow wrote in 1829. To understand why Longfellow came to write *Poems on Slavery*, one must begin in that year, 1829, and track Longfellow's developing thoughts on education and the human soul, which blossomed, at last, into a truly political poetry.

"THE SOUL"

Attendees of the Bowdoin college commencement service in spring 1829 would have been treated to an address by the newly instated modern languages professor, Henry Wadsworth Longfellow. Just a few years earlier, Henry had been a student at Bowdoin, and distinguished himself as having a gift for languages. After graduation Longfellow was hired to create a modern languages department at his *alma mater*. This he did, writing some of the first modern languages textbooks in American history. For his 1829 commencement speech, Longfellow presented a long poem called "The Past and the Present," which proved so popular that he was asked to present the same poem at the Phi Beta Kappa meeting at Bowdoin in 1832 and at Harvard in 1833. This poem—which I will refer to as the Phi Beta Kappa poem—is Longfellow's first major work in verse, but it remains something of a mystery. Though his friends and admirers urged him to publish it, Longfellow never did, and it remains unpublished in its entirety even today. But fortunately, in 1834 and 1835, Longfellow did select a few short sections of it and published them in periodicals. One selection in particular, titled "The Soul," gives us a glimpse into Longfellow's perspective on education in the early 1830s:

> And is this education? This the training
>   Of an immortal spirit for the skies?
> Would you thus teach it virtue, by restraining
>   Its heavenward aspirations till it dies?

> Thus fit it for a life beyond the grave,
>   By making it a helot and a slave
>
> To earth-born passions, and unholy lust,
>   And grovelling appetites? Oh no! The soul,
> Blazoned with shame, and foul with earthly dust,
>   And for an emblem bearing o'er the whole
> The crafty serpent, not the peaceful dove,
> Has no escutcheon for the courts above.
>
> Why, then, prove false to Nature's noblest trust?
>   Why thus restrain the spirit's upward flight,
> And make its dwelling in the loathsome dust,
>   Until th'earth's shadow hath eclipsed its light?
> Why deck the flesh,—the sensual slave of sin,
> And leave in rags the immortal guest within?
>
> Beware! The Israelite of old, who tore
>   The lion in his path, when poor and blind,
> He saw the blessed light of heaven no more,—
>   Shorn of his noble strength, and forced to grind
> In prison, and at times led forth to be
> A pander to Philistine revelry,—
>
> Destroyed himself, and with him those that made
>   A cruel mockery of his sightless eyes!
> So, too, the immortal soul, when once betrayed
>   To minister to lusts it doth despise,
> A poor, blind slave—the scoff and jest of all,—
> Expires,—and thousands perish in the fall![2]

Longfellow here presents a broad, metaphysically informed vision of education. Education should be concerned, he suggests, with "virtue," with "training / of an immortal spirit for the skies." But he sees contemporary education concerned instead with base appetites and worldly vanities. And he issues a warning: just as Samson "destroyed" those that enslaved him, those that force the human soul to remain concerned with earthly desires may be destroyed by the souls that they thus enslave. This poem is surprising in its

---

2. Longfellow, "Soul," 71.

extremes of vision. The human soul is made to aspire not just to be a good citizen or an ethical role model, but to aspire "heavenward." Further, the soul that is disallowed such aspiration will not just be pitiable, but will cause the destruction and ruin of "thousands." That Longfellow chose a figure from the Old Testament to illustrate his musing on education is telling: Longfellow had been raised in a pious, Bible-reading Unitarian household, and the founding pastor of American Unitarianism, William Ellery Channing, was a family friend. Further, Samson is an important figure in English poetic history: John Milton, inspired by Gregory Nazianzus, chose Samson as the tragic hero of his late masterpiece *Samson Agonistes*.

"The Soul" was published in the *Knickerbocker* magazine in January 1835. That same year Harvard University asked Longfellow to be their new chair of modern languages. In order to prepare for his new teaching position, Harvard funded a European trip for Longfellow and his wife, Mary. But on the trip, as Longfellow familiarized himself with the Scandinavian languages he would soon teach at Harvard, his wife became very ill. Here are Longfellow's own words from his journal:

> November 28th, 1835: I am grieved to say that Mary is not so well to-day. She is very feeble, and the physicians tell me that her situation is dangerous. My anxiety is very great. She suffers no pain, and is perfectly calm, but does not regain her strength.[3]

What Henry does not say in this journal entry is that Mary was suffering from complications in the aftermath of a miscarriage. The doctors could do little to help her, and she passed away the next day.

Devastated, Longfellow returned to Cambridge and threw himself into his new teaching job. We can see in his early Harvard lectures that questions of education, literature, and eternity were still on his mind:

> Different characters of books: some instruct us; others educate us. Differences between instruction and

---

3. Longfellow, *Life of Longfellow*, 218.

<u>education</u>, in themselves and in their effects. Learning is the result of instruction; – wisdom, the result of education. There are learned men who are not wise, and wise men who are not learned. And so of books. Some make us learned; others, wise. Some fill the mind with instruction; others develop its powers and resources, and it is filled with wisdom. Instruction is the material – wisdom the result of the mind's operation on that material.

Again; – you may fill a man's body with food, and yet not nourish him. So you may fill his mind with instruction and yet not educate him. – Instruction, then, is the food of the mind; – wisdom is food, changed by the operation of the mind – assimilated to its own nature – and made a part of the mind itself.

This is the difference between instruction and education; between a learned man, and an educated man. We may, however, reduce these principles of criticism to two.

I.
The author's intention in writing the book; – in other words the Class of works to which it belongs. The book is good or bad as a work of art. It is absurd to find fault with a song because it is not a sermon; or a ballad because it is not an epic poem. The question is, Has the author done in a masterly style what he intended to do?

II.
But there is a higher standard than this. A Book may be exquisite as a work of art, and yet in every other point of view execrable. The sculptured vases from Pompeii – the brazen lamps, the reliefs in marble, – looked upon merely as works of art are surpassingly beautiful: yet in themselves – in the scenes they represent how disgusting! – How offensive to the principles of moral delicacy within us!

This higher standard, then, is the Moral Principle of our own Nature as established by Christianity. Christianity is either nothing to us – or it is everything. Therefore I say even in literary criticism, – "grieve not the Spirit" – Whatever offends the Moral Principle is wrong – is bad. It cannot educate us aright.

> The Books, then, that educate us, I prize more highly than those which merely instruct. Books which excite, and develop our minds, which call forth energies in us, of whose existence we hardly dream, which open to us new realms of thought and whisper to our souls, "ye, too, are denizens of these fair lands:" – such books are to be our bosom friends.[4]

These remarks, from Longfellow's 1838 lecture "On the Lives of Literary Men," give us a more detailed, critical explanation of Longfellow's "heavenward" theory of education from "The Soul." True education is the assimilation of learning into our own nature, the changing of bare information into a permanent part of ourselves. Education thus fundamentally changes the soul. To be educated by books that have a mere "masterly style" but lack, or have twisted, moral principles, is to assimilate immorality into one's soul. But to be educated by good books is to make the moral principles of Christianity a permanent part of one's being; to take on, within, the shape of a Christian. Little research has been done on Longfellow's metaphysics of education, but "The Soul" and "The Lives of Literary Men" are, I argue, two great places to begin.

As Longfellow was composing this lecture, he also began to compose what would be his first internationally renowned poems. In moments of quiet reflection, once the cares of his professorship were put away for the day, Longfellow was still a deeply lonely and sad man. Out of his grief, he rallied a cry in verse:

> Tell me not, in mournful numbers,
>   Life is but an empty dream!—
> For the soul is dead the slumbers,
>   And things are not what they seem.
>
> Life is real! Life is earnest!
>   And the grave is not its goal;
> Dust thou art, to dust returnest,
>   Was not spoken of the soul.[5]

---

4. Longfellow, "Lives of Literary Men," 27–33.
5. Longfellow, *Complete Poetical Works*, 3.

From "The Soul" to "The Warning"

In these first two stanzas of his poem "A Psalm of Life" Longfellow employs a similar metaphysics to "The Soul." Primary to this metaphysics is a basic distinction between the nature of the body, which is made to return to dust, and the nature of the soul, which is not. He continues:

> Not enjoyment, and not sorrow,
> Is our destined end or way;
> But to act, that each tomorrow
> Find us farther than to-day.[6]

Instead of an epicurean pursuit of enjoyment (which, as Longfellow reminds us in "The Soul," can turn into lustful hedonism), the purpose of the life of the soul is *action*, particularly action that results in progress. These lines also can be read as having implications for the activity of education, wherein the soul is ethically formed.

In the last stanza of the poem, Longfellow concludes:

> Let us, then, be up and doing,
> With a heart for any fate;
> Still achieving, still pursuing,
> Learn to labor and to wait.[7]

Far from a trite conclusion that the road away from despair is easy, Longfellow is honest with us: work and patience are what we are called to. But he also assures us that such action will "find us farther than" the day before.

From as far away as France, Longfellow received plaudits for his "Psalm of Life," especially his themes of rallying from despair and finding hope in the soul's labor. Closer to home, Nathaniel Hawthorne wrote of his poems that "nothing equal to some of them was ever written in this world,—this western world, I mean; and it would not hurt my conscience much to include the other hemisphere."[8] Longfellow could have gone on writing new variations on his early poems and made a decent poetic career,

---

6. Longfellow, *Complete Poetical Works*, 3.

7. Longfellow, *Complete Poetical Works*, 4.

8. Longfellow, *Life of Longfellow*, 349.

at least for a decade or so. In "A Psalm of Life" and related poems Longfellow had invented a new tone and style for American poetry, one that would put the United States on the literary map of the world. Together with Ralph Waldo Emerson, Edgar Allen Poe, and Nathaniel Hawthorne, Longfellow's first poems helped to launch the renaissance of American literature. But America did not only need metaphysical psalms. Something much more painful and pressing needed addressing.

SLAVERY

In 1835, while Longfellow was living through personal tragedy in Europe, his old family friend William E. Channing published a book called *Slavery*. Though today Channing's overall congenial tone in the book comes across as far too tame, in its time the book seemed radical, especially to the many Northerners who avoided the topic of slavery out of distaste or embarrassment:

> The deliberate, solemn conviction of good men through the world, that slavery is a grievous wrong to human nature, will make itself felt. To increase this moral power is every man's duty. To embody and express this great truth is in every man's power; and thus every man can do something to break the chain of the slave. There are not a few persons, who, from vulgar modes of thinking, cannot be interested in this subject. Because the slave is a degraded being, they think slavery a low topic, and wonder how it can excite the attention and sympathy of those who can discuss or feel for any thing else. Now the truth is, that slavery, regarded only in a philosophical light, is a theme worthy of the highest minds. It involves the gravest questions about human nature and society. It carries us into the problems which have exercised for ages the highest understandings. It calls us to inquire into the foundation, nature, and extent of human rights, into the distinction between a person and a thing, into the true relations of man to man, into the obligations of the community to each of its members, into the ground and laws of property, and, above all, into the true dignity

and indestructible claims of a moral being. I venture to say, there is no subject, now agitated by the community, which can compare in philosophical dignity with slavery; and yet to multitudes the question falls under the same contempt with the slave himself.[9]

By the early 1840s, Longfellow had read Channing's arguments, and they began to work in him. Longfellow had never been a proponent of slavery, but he had also hitherto never published anything about the topic. That was about to change.

In 1842 Longfellow's health had been bad for a long time, and Harvard gave him a sabbatical to go to Germany so that he could undergo a water cure. Whether Longfellow's bathing in the icy cold German waters helped his health, it is difficult to say. But what is certain is that by the time he boarded the ship back to America, he was ready to try something new in poetry. As if reading Channing had not been enough, Longfellow had become friends, in Germany, with the poet Ferdinand Freiligrath, who was appalled at the institution of slavery and heartily encouraged Longfellow's latent abolitionism. When Longfellow was waiting in London for his ship home, he also visited with the young English novelist Charles Dickens, who had just published an essay on slavery in his book *American Notes*. Longfellow wrote to the abolitionist senator Charles Sumner about Dickens's essay: "I have read Dicken[s]'s book. It is jovial and good-natured, and at times very severe. You will read it with delight, and for the most part approbation. He has a grand chapter on Slavery."[10]

Dickens's chapter is a fierce and pointed condemnation of America. In it, Dickens records newspaper stories from America in which the abuses of slaves are detailed not by abolitionists, but by slaveholders themselves, such as: "'Ran away, a black girl, named Mary. Has a scar on her cheek, and the end of one of her toes cut off.'"[11] Dickens muses about what the effect of such brutal treatment of slaves must have on the slave holders and their families:

9. Channing, *Slavery*, 7–8.
10. Longfellow, *Letters*, 473.
11. Dickens, *American Notes*, 163.

> Do we not know that the man who has been born and bred among its wrongs; who has seen in his childhood husbands obliged at the word of command to flog their wives; women, indecently compelled to hold up their own garments that men might lay the heavier stripes upon their legs . . . who has read in youth, and seen his virgin sisters read, descriptions of runaway men and women, and their disfigured persons, which could not be published elsewhere, of so much stock upon a farm, or at a show of beasts:—do we not know that that man, whenever his wrath is kindled up, will be a brutal savage?[12]

Dickens here speaks of another type of education: the education of the white southern youth who grows up witnessing the brutality of slavery. Such an education will shape these youths into brutes, Dickens suggests, for they have witnessed the daily treatment of fellow humans as animals—"so much stock"—or even worse. In his closing paragraph, Dickens links the brutality of slavery with the threat of civil war:

> When knives are drawn by Englishmen in conflict let it be said and known: "We owe this change to Republican slavery. These are the weapons of Freedom. With sharp points and edges such as these, Liberty in America hews and hacks her slaves; or, failing that pursuit, her sons devote them to a better use, and turn them on each other."[13]

Thus, the cruelty of slavery spills over, from violent treatment of the enslaved to violent treatment of the free, and from the American scene to England—England, who can blame American "Liberty" for providing them with an example of how to treat their fellows. This "Liberty" makes a mockery of itself, destroying enslaved and free alike. These are the arguments that Longfellow called "grand," and they worked within him on the boat home from England.

---

12. Dickens, *American Notes*, 168.
13. Dickens, *American Notes*, 169.

From "The Soul" to "The Warning"

"THE WARNING"

In a letter to his father, Longfellow writes: "On the passage home I wrote some poems on Slavery, which I shall publish shortly in a pamphlet."[14] This pamphlet, titled *Poems on Slavery*, contains seven new poems: The first is a sort of hymn in praise of Channing's abolitionist writings. Several other of the poems are portraits of the sorrows and hopes of enslaved men. One celebrates the liberation of slaves by a remorseful slave-owner. Perhaps the most devastating, "The Quadroon Girl" describes a poor man selling his weeping daughter to a slave trader. But the eighth and last poem in the collection, "The Warning," was not, in fact, a new poem at all:

> Beware! The Israelite of old, who tore
>   The lion in his path,—when, poor and blind,
> He saw the blessed light of heaven no more,
>   Shorn of his noble strength and forced to grind
> In prison, and at last led forth to be
> A pander to Philistine revelry,—
>
> Upon the pillars of the temple laid
>   His desperate hands, and in its overthrow
> Destroyed himself, and with him those who made
>   A cruel mockery of his sightless woe;
> The poor, blind Slave, the scoff and jest of all,
> Expired, and thousands perished in the fall!
>
> There is a poor, blind Samson in this land,
>   Shorn of his strength, and bound in bonds of steel,
> Who may, in some grim revel, raise his hand,
>   And shake the pillars of this Commonweal,
> Till the vast Temple of our liberties
> A shapeless mass of wreck and rubbish lies.[15]

Astute readers of Longfellow would have recognized this as a revision of the final stanzas of his 1835 poem "The Soul." But gone are the final lines about the destruction of the human soul through

---

14. Longfellow, *Letters*, 476.
15. Longfellow, *Complete Poetical Works*, 28.

worldly desires and improper education. Instead we find a new analogue for Samson: the American slave, who, because of the injustices done to him, threatens the country. Longfellow has both heightened the political stakes of the poem and the detail from the book of Judges. We now see the "pillars of the temple" of the Philistines compared with the "pillars" of the American "commonweal." Further, we have the added emotional image of Sampson's "desperate hands." Just as, in "The Soul," those who force the human soul to indulge in lusts unworthy of it are, by implication, responsible for their own destruction, so too those who keep the American slave in chains seem, by implication, responsible for their own wreck and ruin. And it is telling that Longfellow includes "our liberties" among those things that are wrecked. Following Dickens's arguments, Longfellow implies that to keep a human soul in chains is not merely an offense against that human, but also an offense against the very concept of liberty which the nation hypocritically claims to hold most dear.[16]

The responses to Longfellow's *Poems on Slavery* were swift, vehement, and polarized. The outspoken abolitionist John Greenleaf Whittier was so impressed, he sent a letter to Longfellow offering

---

16. At this point it is worth pausing to point out that Longfellow's rewriting of "The Soul" as "The Warning" has not been sufficiently acknowledged in the critical literature. In a previous paper "On the Origin of Longfellow's 'The Warning,'" I pointed out that the major Longfellow critics of the twentieth century are misleading at best on the origin of "The Warning." In 1938 Lawrence Thompson acknowledges that "The Warning" was taken from the Phi Beta Kappa poem, but he describes it as from a section hitherto unpublished before 1842 (Thompson, *Young Longfellow*, 202). He does mention "The Soul," but describes it as a wholly separate poem from "The Warning." In 2003 Robert Gale, perhaps relying on Thompson, further bungles the account, describing "The Soul" and "The Warning" as different poems, and implying that "The Soul" was never published (Gale, *Henry Wadsworth Longfellow Companion*, 191). But the story does not end here—I have subsequently found that at least one critic before now has correctly identified "The Warning" as a rewrite of "The Soul": Janet Harris, who in 1978 acknowledges that "The Warning . . . was taken, in part from The Soul, which appeared in the Knickerbocker magazine" (Harris, "Longfellow's Poems on Slavery," 85). Harris, then, should be considered the one reliable source on the relationship between "The Warning" and the Phi Beta Kappa poem, and Thompson and Gale as unfortunately unreliable.

to nominate him for a seat in congress. Abolitionist newspapers republished the poems and were effusive about their importance. Southern newspapers declined to even review the collection due to their rules about never letting the word *slavery* appear in print. Poe, an outspoken critic of abolition, was disgusted with the collection and wrote that he dismissed Longfellow's whole project "with no more profound feeling than that of contempt."[17] Longfellow's personal friends seem at times confused about his choice of subject: "I was never more surprised than at you writing poems about Slavery," Nathaniel Hawthorne wrote to him. "You have never poetized a practical subject hitherto."[18] Other friends questioned whether his condemnation of Slavery was wise, or whether he blew the plight of the slave out of proportion. "I pity the masters more than the slaves," wrote one friend, who had just spent some time in the south.[19]

Longfellow did not bend on the slavery issue: in letter after letter, he defends his choice of subject as both proper and right. But he also rejected Whittier's offer of a political career. While his subject in *Poems on Slavery* was a pointed and pressing political issue, his project was no less poetic than it was practical. What he had done in *Poems on Slavery*, and in "The Warning" in particular, was apply his metaphysical convictions to practical politics. If life is not an empty dream, if the soul is dead that slumbers, then the emptiness and forced slumber of the soul that slavery imposes is antithetical to the whole purpose of human life, and the slave holder is the extreme opposite of the true educator that Longfellow envisions. The slave holder holds the human soul back, forcibly, from learning and flourishing, from its heavenward call to wisdom. This principle would be confirmed by Frederick Douglass a year later in his *Narrative of the Life of a Slave*. In Douglass's story of his boyhood, he describes an epiphany he had when his master forbade him from learning how to read:

17. Poe, "Review of Longfellow, *Poems*," 133.
18. Longfellow, *Life of Longfellow*, 450.
19. Longfellow, *Life of Longfellow*, 449.

> I now understood what had been to me a most perplexing difficulty—to wit, the white man's power to enslave the black man. It was a grand achievement, and I prized it highly. From that moment, I understood the pathway from slavery to freedom.... Though conscious of the difficulty of learning without a teacher, I set out with a high hope, and a fixed purpose, at whatever cost of trouble, to learn how to read.[20]

To write about education and the human soul in nineteenth-century America, then, was to write about subjects that had tremendous bearing on the question of slavery. To conclude, as Longfellow did, that the human soul is made for the wisdom acquired by true education is to imply that slavery is a gross injustice and a crime against humanity. Longfellow, in time, recognized this, and sought to do it justice in his verse.

---

20. Douglass, *Narrative*, 33.

7

Prudentius among the Moderns
The Cathemerinon Hymns in the Work of C. S. Lewis and T. S. Eliot

THE DECADES-LONG DIALOGUE ON literature between C. S. Lewis and T. S. Eliot is instructive: these literary minds batted back and forth over their readings of Dante, *Hamlet*, and *Paradise Lost*, not to mention the state of modern poetry; these matches have been noted and debated.[1] But what is less documented is their mutual admiration for the fifth-century Christian poet Prudentius as a master of lyric poetry; further, both Lewis and Eliot borrowed Prudentius's imaginative descriptions of the holiness of heaven in their own writings. In this essay I explore the relationship that Eliot and Lewis had with the writings of Prudentius and give account of how Prudentius came to influence them and thus remain relevant over fifteen centuries after he wrote.

Though he is considered the greatest Latin poet of his age,[2] we know little about Prudentius. By his own rather vague attestation, he had a career as a Roman official in the second half of

---

1. For an overview of this dialogue, and a lively corrective of a reductive view of it, see Huttar, "C. S. Lewis's Appreciation," 265–84. Further, I am grateful to Dr. Huttar for his feedback on an early draft of this chapter.
2. Prudentius, *Poems*, ix.

the fourth century AD.³ After rising through the ranks of power in Hispania, Prudentius says that he visited Rome just after the turn of the century. In 405, he published his impressively varied body of verse, which includes the *Cathemerinon* hymns and the *Psychomachia*, an allegorical epic that describes a battle between personified virtues and vices.⁴ Little more is known of his life, and yet his poems have proved immortal.

ELIOT AND PRUDENTIUS

Prudentius has enjoyed some sort of canonical status ever since he wrote; both his *Cathemerinon* and his *Psychomachia* were influential on all subsequent Western hymnography and epic,⁵ and by the early twentieth century he was seen as a minor but not forgettable figure.⁶ In 1921 we begin to see a hopeful new discussion of Prudentius. C. S. Lewis was still an undergraduate at Oxford then, but T. S. Eliot was fresh off his second collection of poems and had already begun work on *The Waste Land*. In a letter to Richard Aldington in November 1921, while expressing doubts about the poetry of his fellow modernist H. D., Eliot associates his own early work with Prudentius:

> Morally, I find a neurotic carnality [in H. D.'s poems] which I dislike. (I imagine you dislike equally the Prudentianism of myself and Mr. Joyce, and expect you

---

3. In fact, despite his early date, Prudentius was the second major Iberian writer in Christian literature, the first being Juvencus, who flourished in the reign of Constantine and around 330 published the first New Testament Latin epic, the *Liber Evangeliorum*.

4. Quasten, *Patrology*, 4:281.

5. Rand, "Prudentius and Christian Humanism," 81–83; also see Lewis's remarks on the influence of *Psychomachia* in *The Allegory of Love*, discussed below.

6. In his 1920 article on Prudentius, Edward Rand, for instance, writes: "Prudentius is not among the great writers; his versatility interfered with the attainment of something really great. But among the lesser lights his eminence is incontestable; if Plautus, Propertius, and Juvenal deserve the title of classical, so does Prudentius." Rand, "Prudentius and Christian Humanism," 83.

to abhor the poem on which I have been working and which I am taking with me!).⁷

The poem Eliot refers to here is the early draft of *The Waste Land* poem, which he had been working on that fall while at Margate.

A year later, Eliot would write, again to Aldington, that he wanted to borrow a copy of J. P. Migne's critical edition of Prudentius's poems in Latin.⁸ This borrowing of Prudentius may have been to help Eliot prepare his Clark Lectures, which he delivered at Cambridge in 1926.

In the Clark lectures, Eliot explains his dissatisfaction with the devotional verse of the Victorians:

> I used to think that my inability to feel devotional verse—such as that of Christina Rossetti, who is a diluted Theresa—was due to the weakness of my own flesh and spirit; but that was before I had read the *Paradiso*, or any of the Latin Hymns from Prudentius to Aquinas.... One of the reasons for the general inferiority, or let us say less positively, of the general unsatisfactoriness, of the devotional verse of the last three hundred years, [is] this substitution of the divine passion by the human. Instead of being presented with a new passion, we find only the old watered down."⁹

Against this watered-down devotional verse Eliot pits the hymns of Prudentius and his medieval inheritors Thomas Aquinas and Dante. In 1929 we again see evidence of Eliot's ongoing preference for Prudentius, this time in a review of Paul Rand's *Founders of the Middle Ages*. Eliot praises Rand's chapter "On the New Poetry" as "mainly a defence and exposition—and a persuasive one—of the poetry of Prudentius."¹⁰ Thus from 1921 to 1929 we have clear evidence that Eliot read Prudentius's poems and critical writings about them, that he promoted the poems of Prudentius to others

---

7. Eliot, *Letters*, 1:606.
8. Eliot, *Letters*, 2:793.
9. Eliot, *Varieties of Metaphysical Poetry*, 167.
10. Eliot, *Complete Prose*, 589.

in lectures and reviews, and that he associated his own poetry with that of Prudentius.

To my knowledge there has been no critical effort to explore the verse of Eliot in light of the hymns of Prudentius to see what, if any, influence can be ascertained. Several scholars have drawn connections between the two poets, but never with an eye toward direct influence.[11] But given Eliot's remarks of the 1920s, I propose two possible instances of Prudentian influence on Eliot's early poem "The Hippopotamus," published in *Poems* (1920).

"The Hippopotamus" is written in rhyming quatrains of iambic tetrameter. In the first six stanzas, Eliot contrasts "the broadbacked hippopotamus," who is "merely flesh and blood," is "feeble," and whose "voice / Betrays inflexions hoarse and odd," with the "True Church," who "can never fail, for it is based upon the rock."[12] But in the last three stanzas, both the hippopotamus and the church experience an unexpected change of fortunes:

> I saw the 'potamus take wing
> Ascending from the damp savannas
> And quiring round him angels sing
> The praise of God, in loud hosannas.
>
> Blood of the Lamb shall wash him clean
> And him shall heavenly arms enfold,
> Among the saints he shall be seen
> Performing on a harp of gold.
>
> He shall be washed as white as snow,
> By all the martyr virgins kissed
> While the True Church remains below
> Wrapt in the old Miasmal mist.[13]

---

11. See O'Daly, *Days Linked by Song,* 286; and Cotten, "Eliot's *The Wasteland,*" 10. O'Daly, for instance, points out that both Prudentius in one of his hymns and Eliot in "Ash Wednesday" use imagery of dry bones coming back to life found in Ezek 37:3–4. However, O'Daly does not suggest direct influence of Prudentius's writings upon Eliot's poetry.

12. Eliot, *Poems,* 27.

13. Eliot, *Poems,* 28.

This assumption into heaven and purification of the hippopotamus parallels imagery in the twenty-first and twenty-fifth stanzas of Prudentius's first hymn in the *Cathemerinon*, which is also written in iambic tetrameter quatrains:

> To Jesus let us lift our souls
> In prayers and tears and holy thoughts;
> For fervent supplication keeps
> The pure of heart from bonds of sleep.
>
> Come thou, oh Christ, and banish sleep;
> Break through the chains that night has forged
> And wash away our ancient stain;
> Renew the light within our souls.[14]

Especially evident in both Eliot and Prudentius are images of ascent toward heaven and the washing clean of the ascending one. Further, both contrast this ascension and purification with being trapped and blinded below. Whereas Prudentius seems to be beseeching Christ on behalf of Christian believers in general, Eliot cynically leaves the "True Church" below in "Miasmal mist," and it is only the unlikely hippopotamus who leaves the "damp savannas" and becomes the recipient of what Prudentius requests.[15] Given that in 1921 Eliot explicitly named his poetry "Prudentian," I argue that in both the poem's iambic tetrameter form and its closing imagery we are seeing the evidence of Prudentianism.[16]

---

14. Prudentius, *Poems*, 7–8.

15. Lest there were any doubt, Eliot explained in 1953 that "It is about the Church of England . . . no one else need be offended." Eliot, *Poems*, 523.

16. While Eliot's characteristic irony is present, I believe we also see Eliot's eschewing of what he calls "substitution of the divine passion by the human" in his 1926 Lectures. The hippopotamus's ascension and purification, like that of the believer in Prudentius's first hymn, is not described primarily in the romantic or erotic terms (though the poem is not devoid of such language) used by Saint Teresa or Christina Rosetti. In fact, the reigning imagery in both is that of the unholy darkness and mist of night being replaced by the holy, purifying light and heat of the sun. I will return at the end of this chapter to the implications that this has for our understanding of holiness in Prudentius and Eliot.

In all, Eliot includes seven poems in iambic tetrameter quatrains in his *Poems* (1920), two of which, "The Hippopotamus" and "Mr. Eliot's Sunday Morning Service," are explicitly concerned with theological subjects. Early drafts of *The Waste Land* reveal that a large portion of "The Fire Sermon" continued in this quatrain style, though in it Eliot added a fifth iambic foot to each line.[17] What remains the same as the quatrains in *Poems* (1920) is the rhyming of the first and third, and second and fourth lines. In his notes to Eliot on this quatrain, Pound writes: "verse not interesting enough as verse to warrant so much of it."[18] Further, Pound crossed out the last foot in the first and third lines, reducing them to tetrameter. In the final version of *The Waste Land*, the rhyming quatrains have become:

> The typist home at teatime, clears her breakfast, lights
> Her stove and lays out food in tins.[19]

Eliot, on Pound's recommendation, condensed a longer "prudentian" passage into two unrhymed lines of iambic verse that appear in a long, unbroken stanza. Thankfully, later in the same stanza, Eliot does retain some end rhymes from the earlier rhymed-quatrain version.

Thus the Prudentian form so apparent in the 1920 *Poems*'s quatrains becomes less apparent in the final version of *The Waste Land*, but the early drafts show us that Eliot employed it as late as November 1921 when he was working on the poem in Margate. Jeffrey Perl has called attention to Pound's description of Eliot's quatrains as reminiscent of the "'Bay State Hymn Book' . . . omitting rhyme in the first and third lines of each stanza, as American hymns, with relative insouciance of style, were free to do."[20] Like-

---

17. See Eliot, *Waste Land*, 44–45.
18. Eliot, *Waste Land*, 44–45.
19. Eliot, *Waste Land*, 32–33.
20. Perl, "Disambivalent Quatrains," 137. Perl further explains that Pound in this section compares Eliot with the French poet Gautier, as both poets sought to embrace a more formal verse after what they saw as the abuses of *vers libre*. Further, Gautier also wrote a poem in tetrameter on a hippopotamus, but it lacks any religious themes or imagery. See Eliot, *Poems*, 522.

wise, Christopher Ricks and Jim McCue describe Eliot's "The Hippopotamus" as "hymnal."[21] But what none of these commentators account for is that the tetrameter quatrain hymn, from American hymns to the French poet Gautier to Eliot, all rely on Prudentius as their early Latin model, and that in 1921 Eliot explicitly calls his own poetry "Prudentian."

LEWIS AND PRUDENTIUS

More study is required to suss out the extent of Prudentianism in Eliot's *Poems* (1920) and *The Waste Land*. For our present purposes, it is sufficient to say that Eliot helped to place Prudentius in the literary air—so to speak—of England in the 1920s. Thus when C. S. Lewis came of age as a critic it should not be so surprising that Prudentius became a concern. Lewis is, in fact, much more explicit about his debt to and struggle with Prudentius than is Eliot. We see this especially in two of Lewis's works: *The Allegory of Love* (1936), and *The Great Divorce* (1945).

The Allegory of Love was C. S. Lewis's first major literary-critical monograph, and established him as a keen critic of Medieval poetry. In the book, Lewis tracks the development of allegory in Western literature, devoting space to Prudentius's *Psychomachia*. His estimation of it is measured to say the least:

> The historian is not at liberty to dispose his fable as he would wish. If, in fact, the mountains travailed and a mouse was born, his narrative must be content with the anti-climax. Such an anti-climax has to be faced when we reach the fully fledged allegorical poem, the *Pyschomachia* of Prudentius. It is unworthy of the great utterances that lead up to it and explain its existence.[22]

---

21. Eliot, *Poems*, 525.
22. Lewis, *Allegory of Love*, 83.

Thus, Lewis says, "it is possible to overrate the *Psychomachia*. If Prudentius had not written it, another would. It is a symptom rather than a source."[23] Lewis explains:

> The *Psychomachia* fails, partly because Prudentius is naturally a lyrical and reflective poet . . . to whom the epic manner comes with difficulty, and partly for a different reason. While it is true that the *bellum intestinum* is the root of all allegory, it is no less true that only the crudest allegory will represent it by a pitched battle.[24]

Lewis quotes a dozen or so lines from Prudentius's description of gory battle between the personified virtues and vices, estimating some as more successful than others, but concluding that "it is only when Prudentius turns away from the actual fighting that his allegory begins to convince us."[25] Lewis praises highly "a single sentence," toward the end of the poem, which he says "comes from the heart and reveals in a flash the real genesis of the poem":[26]

> War rages, horrid war
> Even in our bones; our double nature sounds
> With armed discord.[27]

"It was," Lewis writes, "no prosaic desire for innocent epic that moved Prudentius to write, and his contemporaries to read, the *Psychomachia*. It was their daily and hourly experience of the *non simplex natura*."[28] Though Lewis begins his discussion of Prudentius rather coolly, reminding us repeatedly that *Psychomachia* is, especially in its literal descriptions of battle, no great poem, he ends by praising Prudentius's thought, namely that human nature is, in this life, the primary site of conflict between virtue and vice, between the holy and the unholy.

---

23. Lewis, *Allegory of Love*, 84.
24. Lewis, *Allegory of Love*, 86.
25. Lewis, *Allegory of Love*, 89.
26. Lewis, *Allegory of Love*, 91.
27. Lewis, *Allegory of Love*, 91. This is Lewis's own translation.
28. Lewis, *Allegory of Love*, 91.

After *The Allegory of Love*, one might not expect Lewis to return to Prudentius: his remarks about Prudentius's success as an epic poet are, after all, as disparaging as Eliot's are laudatory. But in Lewis's nod to Prudentius's skill as a lyric poet, we see the seed of what would blossom into not just influence, but inspiration. In 1945, Prudentius appears again in Lewis's published work, this time in the *Guardian* newspaper, in the middle of a serialized novella, *Who Goes Home? Or The Grand Divorce*, which would later be published as *The Great Divorce: A Dream*.[29] After boarding a mysterious bus in a "grey town,"[30] an unnamed narrator is taken to a "level grassy country through which there ran a wide river," where the ghostly spirits of the damned and the shining spirits of the blessed are allowed to meet and talk.[31] The narrator, who we realize must be among the damned, meets the blessed spirit of George MacDonald, who acts as a sort of Dantean guide through this strange borderland of the afterlife.

As the narrator questions MacDonald about the fate of the damned ghosts, Prudentius is brought into the conversation:

> "Did ye never hear of the *Refrigerium*? A man with your advantages might have read of it in Prudentius, not to mention Jeremy Taylor."
> "The name is familiar, Sir, but I'm afraid I've forgotten what it means."
> "It means that the damned have holidays—excursions, ye understand."[32]

Walter Hooper, among others, reports that Lewis had been contemplating the idea of *Refrigerium* since at least 1931. Instead of Prudentius, Hooper primarily credits Jeremy Taylor:

> Taylor, whose *Works* Arthur Greeves had given [Lewis] in August 1931. As he was reading the books during September '31, it was probably then that he came upon

---

29. Zaleski and Zaleski, *Fellowship*, 315.
30. Lewis, *Great Divorce*, 8.
31. Lewis, *Great Divorce*, 19.
32. Lewis, *Great Divorce*, 67–68.

The Poets and the Fathers

[this] passage in Taylor's sermon.... 'The Church of Rome amongst other strange opinions hath inserted this one into her public offices; that the perishing souls in hell may have sometimes remission and refreshment, like the fits of an intermitting fever.'[33]

Two years later this seed of an idea blossomed into a book project:

> On Easter Sunday Lewis has an idea for a book (probably while in Church) which he outlines to [his brother] Warren, who records it in his diary: 'A religious work, based on the opinion of some of the Fathers, that while punishment for the damned is eternal, it is intermittent; he proposes to do sort of an infernal day excursion to Paradise.'[34]

By the spring of 1944, Lewis was reading chapters from the book to the Inklings. Tolkien records in his journals, "I do not think so well of a chapter of C. S. L's new moral allegory or 'vision,' based on the medieval fancy of the Refrigerium, by which lost souls have an occasional holiday in Paradise."[35]

What neither Warren nor Tolkien explicitly states is that the idea of *refrigerium* was found by Lewis in Prudentius above all. The character of MacDonald himself in *The Great Divorce* credits Prudentius with the idea, as does Jeremy Taylor, who quotes Prudentius's fifth hymn in the *Cathemerinon*, *Hymnus ad inscensum lucernae*, or "Hymn for the Lighting of the Lamps." And we know from the *Allegory of Love* that Lewis had spent a good deal of time in the mid-1930s studying the poet's oeuvre.[36] In the passage in

---

33. Hooper, *C. S. Lewis: A Biography*, 220–21.
34. Duriez, *Oxford Inklings*, 240.
35. Quoted in Carter, *Inklings*, 194.
36. Lewis refers specifically to both the *Psychomachia* and the *Hamartigenia* of Prudentius in *Allegory of Love*. Though he does not mention the *Cathemerinon* by name, it is reasonable to expect him to have been familiar with the work, as, indeed, George MacDonald expects in *The Great Divorce*. Additionally, Hooper speculates ideas related to *refrigerium* can also be found in two of Lewis's poems of the 1930s. See Hooper, *C. S. Lewis: A Companion & Guide*, 281.

Hymn 5 where *refrigerium* is described, Prudentius is waxing eloquent on "the heavenly realm where the redeemed abide":[37]

> There bright roses exhale fragrance from gardens rare,
> And where murmuring springs water the earth around. . . .
> Here the souls of the blest wandering in grassy meads
> Blend their voices in song, chanting melodious hymns
> That devoutly resound through happy glades,
> And with radiant feet they tread the lilies fair.
>
> Even souls of the lost suffering in depths of Hell
> Have some respite from pain, holding glad holiday
> On that night when the Lord came to the world above
> Up from Acheron's pool, rising to life again. . . .
> Hell's fierce torments subside, bringing surcease from pain
> To the spirits that live ever in penal fires;
> Calm and joy for a while reign in that prison house
> And the sulphurous streams burn not with wonted rage.
>
> Festive vigil Thy flock keeps on this holy night
> Through the hours till the dawn, chanting the praise of God.[38]

The context of the *refrigerium* descriptions is Prudentius's dramatization of the celebrations of the resurrection of Christ in the three realms of heaven, hell, and earth. In heaven, imagined as a place of "bright roses," "grassy meads," and "happy glades," the blessed souls sing, chant, and even dance. In Hell, the souls enjoy a "glad holiday," which consists of "surcease from pain" and a state of "calm and joy." On Earth, the church mimics the blessed in heaven, "chanting the praise of God" in a "festive Vigil."

In *The Great Divorce* Lewis borrows for his narrative purposes the descriptions of both the damned and the blessed in these lines. Indeed, it is the quatrain about the setting of heaven that is most obviously paralleled by Lewis's description toward the end of the book of the procession of the blessed Sarah Smith:

---

37. Prudentius, *Poems*, 36.
38. Prudentius, *Poems*, 36–37.

> All down one long aisle of the forest the undersides of the leafy branches had begun to tremble with dancing light. ... Some kind of procession was approaching us, and the light came from the persons who composed it.
>   First came bright Spirits, not the Spirit of men, who danced and scattered flowers—soundlessly falling, lightly drifting flowers. ... Then on the left and right, at each side of the forest avenue, came youthful shapes, boys upon one hand, and girls upon the other. If I could remember their singing and write down the notes, no man who read that score would ever grow sick or old. Between them went musicians: and after these a lady in whose honour all this was being done.[39]

Though Lewis's style is quite different from that of Prudentius, all the major elements of Prudentius's paradisal descriptions are here: flowers; trees; and processing, singing, dancing, blessed souls.

However, in Prudentius the benefits of the *refrigerium* are just that: a cooling of the hellfire that brings about a temporary rest, peace, and even joy. This rest from torment seems to be the content of the "holiday" that Prudentius imagines. But that word *holiday*, in Latin *celebres*,[40] has put into Lewis's mind not just a rest, but a journey—in this case, an excursion to the "grassy country" of heaven. Prudentius does not imagine this, but rather keeps the celebrants of Christ's resurrection in their proper spheres: the blessed in heaven, the damned in hell, the living on Earth. Lewis boldly puts them all in Prudentius's heaven. For the narrator himself, we learn at the end, has only been dreaming that he is a damned soul. He wakes at the end to realize he is still among the living.[41]

What is Lewis up to here, especially in regard to Prudentius? It is certainly out of our purview to attempt a thorough interpretation of Lewis's theology of the afterlife in *The Great Divorce*. At least we can say that Lewis borrows Prudentius's descriptions of heaven and his concept that the damned have holidays in order to give the living an imaginative exercise: given the choice, would

---

39 Lewis, *Great Divorce*, 117–18.
40 Prudentius, *Poems*, 46.
41 Lewis, *Great Divorce*, 144–46.

one choose the green country and the life of the blessed, or the grey town and the life of the damned? As MacDonald explains in the final scene of the narrator's vision: "Ye saw the choices a bit more clearly than ye could see them on Earth: the lens was clearer. But it was still seen through the lens. . . . The bitter drink of death is still before you. Ye are only dreaming."[42] Literarily, Lewis has repurposed descriptions presented as literal in Prudentius's hymn into an allegorical "lens" through which his readers can see "a bit more clearly" the earthly choices that lead to heaven or hell.

We may now conclude that Eliot and Lewis are joined in both their admiration for Prudentius's lyric poetry and their affinity for his contrasting descriptions of holiness and unholiness in the *Cathemerinon* hymns. In Hymn 1 and Eliot's "Hippopotamus" purification through washing and light are contrasted with imprisoning mist and blinding darkness. In Hymn 5 and Lewis's *Great Divorce* a green place of trees, flowers, and singing, dancing saints is contrasted with a place of dimness. While any number of religious poets have used similar contrasting descriptions of holiness and unholiness, it is significant that both Lewis and Eliot single out Prudentius as an influence on their religious imagery. In so doing, these writers have accomplished the worthy work of keeping the poems and ideas of Prudentius alive and active in the modern age.

---

42. Lewis, *Great Divorce*, 144.

8

Scott Cairns as Syriac Poet
Reading the Eastern in Idiot Psalms

IF IT HAS BECOME cliché to praise the contemporary poet for revealing the extraordinary in the everyday, it has become just as cliché to praise the Christian poet for revealing the holy in the everyday. Reading much of what passes for criticism of Christian poets today, one could be forgiven for concluding that what critics ask of them is that they rewrite "God's Grandeur" *ad nauseam*. But those looking for the sacramental ecstasy of Hopkins or the erotic allegory of Saint John of the Cross will find little of either in Scott Cairns's *Idiot Psalms*. Though, like Dante before him, Cairns fills his poems with pilgrims and repentance, they are always *slow* pilgrims and *late* repentance. If we were to place Cairns's subjects in Dante's cosmos, they would be hanging out in ante-Purgatory, looking at a few more centuries before they could approach Peter's gate.

Much of this slowness and lateness is to be found in Cairns's labored language. Cairns is happy, in "The Fragile Surround," to reword Saint Paul's quick phrase "live and move and have our being" into several lines of verse:

> Availing space in which we live and move,
> and chance to glimpse the trembling import of
> our late, suspected being—[1]

Gerunds, commas, and parentheticals pile up between Cairns's nouns and verbs with such regularity that Nate Klug, in his 2009 review of Cairns's previous collection, *Compass of Affection*, all but accuses Cairns of being embarrassed by his faith. Klug explains that Cairns at times "ends up alienating the reader by providing sloppy witness": "Cairns' sheer talkiness—the constant qualifiers, the self-deprecation manifested as inarticulacy . . . undercuts the compelling narrative and subtle metrics."[2] Who does Klug point to instead as a less hesitant and ingratiating religious poet? Hopkins, of course, as well as Donne, Milton, and Shakespeare himself.[3]

Those who agree with Klug that Cairns is guilty of writing overly talkative, hesitant, and embarrassed poems may have hoped that in his new collection Cairns would have tended more toward those poets of the Western tradition whose bread and butter is, as Klug puts it, descriptions of "a soul drowning in God."[4] But *Idiot Psalms* gives us more of the same Cairns, if a bit more focused and metrically precise. Part of this focus comes from the fact that this new collection is, well, new. Cairns's last two collections, *Compass of Affection* (2006) and *Philokalia* (2002), contained both new and selected poems and, as is often the case with such collections, the new seems a little lost in the selected. Not so in the new collection, where Cairns lets us know what he's been up to for the last eight years in between publishing translations and prose pieces.

Idiot Psalms is built on the backbone of 14 psalms, most of them divided into two or three sections both by stanza breaks and by indentation of each section after its opening, left-aligned line. The psalms are all spoken to God, and contain some of the most honest and bare writing Cairns has yet delivered:

---

1. Cairns, *Slow Pilgrim*, 245.
2. Klug, "Upside of Terror?," 458.
3. Klug, "Upside of Terror?," 457.
4. Klug, "Upside of Terror?," 457.

> My enemies are plentiful, and I
> surround them, these enemies
> camped firmly in my heart, what passes,
> lo these dreary ages, for my heart.[5]

Here is an honest reimagining of King David's real, historical enemies as the troubles and/or vices of the poet's heart. But here, too, is that talkiness, that repetition, with piling qualifiers, of both "enemies" and "my heart," as if Cairns cannot take a break from slow restatement even in his realest moments.

What if instead of asking Cairns—or any contemporary poet of faith, for that matter—to be Hopkins or Donne or—God help us—Shakespeare, we began to take them on their own terms? In the case of Cairns, at least, such a critical move can open up new ways to read the poet's choice of language and choice of form. A biographically obvious but under-acknowledged aspect of Cairns's life and work is that he is an American convert to the Eastern Orthodox faith, and is especially interested in the ancient, Christian Syriac spiritual and poetic tradition. The fact that Cairns is American, and both was educated and is now employed in the American university system, means that he is deeply embedded in the Western poetic tradition, which includes, of course, Hopkins, Donne, Shakespeare, and Dante. But the fact that Cairns is an Eastern Orthodox Christian means that he has slowly, over the past decades, become, by choice and practice, more and more embedded in the Eastern Christian tradition, which includes the poetry of ancient Christianity in its Syriac and Syriac-influenced Greek forms. The two most prominent poets of this tradition are the fourth-century Saint Ephrem the Syrian, who largely invented the Syriac hymnographic tradition, and the sixth-century Saint Romanos the Melodist, who wrote Greek poetry in Syriac metrical forms and invented the kontakion hymn tradition still used in the Orthodox Church the world over. Both poets composed in the Syriac syllabic form, wherein each line of poetry is broken into two or three syllabically precise sections, separated by caesuras.

---

5. Cairns, *Slow Pilgrim*, 248.

In English translation, preserving the syllable count and caesura structure, a typical Syriac stanza by Ephrem would look like this:

> One day I found a pearl.   A mystery was in it
> About God's coming kingdom,   mirrors of his majesty,
> And streams from his only Son.   There I peered, and there I drank.[6]

Here Ephrem employs fourteen-syllable lines, broken by a caesura between the seventh and eighth syllables. Following a similar structure in Greek two centuries later, though including more varied syllable counts, Romanos writes:

> Today the virgin gives birth   to he who is beyond being
>   and in the cave the earth   meets the unreachable heavens;
> Angels above are creating   glory in language,
>   magi below make their journey,   chasing down starlight;
> for through her he   has now been born.
>   Such a small child   is God—who outstrips the ages.[7]

At times Cairns follows quite strictly the formal syllabic structure of the Syriac/Syriac-Greek poetic tradition, as in "Hesychasterion":

> I am etching out a dwelling   in the granite of my heart.
> I am thinking then to torch   its walls and sweep out all debris
> with a green, a heavy branch   of rosemary.[8]

In other poems Cairns mimics the style of many English translations of Ephrem that convert the sections of lines after each caesura into indented second and third lines, as in "To what might this be compared?":

> As one peering, fixed
>   into the icon's
>   limpid eye observes
> A subtle quickening
>   just there, beyond
>   the opaque plane—[9]

---

6. Ephrem the Syrian, "Hymn 1 On the Pearl," ll. 1–3. My translation.

7. Romanos the Melodist, "On the Nativity of Christ," 109.

8. Cairns, *Slow Pilgrim*, 250.

9. Cairns, *Slow Pilgrim*, 255.

Cairns has made it quite clear, moreover, that he is familiar with the Christian Syriac tradition. He included six translations from Saint Ephrem's poems in his 2007 anthology *Love's Immensity: Mystics on the Endless Life*, and Saint Isaac the Syrian, perhaps the greatest prose writer of the Syriac Christian tradition, has appeared on the cover of two of Cairns's last three collections of original verse, including *Idiot Psalms*. Further, Orthodox parishes the world over still sing stanzas from the Kontakia of Saint Romanos on Christmas, the Nativity of the Theotokos, and other major feasts throughout the year.

Added to the formal elements of Eastern Christian poetry in Cairns's work are the elements of Eastern Christian poetry within the content. Cairns's poems are filled with monks, icons, Greek theological terms, and Mount Athos—that island Mecca of the Orthodox world. Further, his language, found by Klug to be overly talky, embarrassed, and ingratiating, often imitates the language of Orthodox spirituality, especially in its slow, deliberate aridity. *Aridity* is a word that is often used in the Orthodox Church to describe the experience of the great fast of Lent, the feeling of being stripped of spiritual luxury and spiritual ease, a word for the desert, both literally and spiritually. Many of Cairns's speakers and characters seem as if they are in deserts, either by necessity or their own choice. Enjoyment of the more arid passages in Cairns is like the enjoyment of Lent: learned, intentional, difficult, and somewhat rare.

And yet, it would be a mistake to read all of Cairns's new poems as exercises in some sort of latter-day desert monasticism. Cairns writes a poetry of ascesis, but it is much more the ascesis of the lay pilgrim, the lay poet, than it is of Dostoyevsky's Elder Zosima, or the monk on Mount Athos. Cairns, for instance, is not ashamed to write of married love, and in a manner that points his readers toward the literal sense of marriage, not the erotic, mystical love between the monk and God. Perhaps this, the quality of lay ascesis in both form and style, is what can be so off-putting about Cairns. He will neither speak the language of the common, carousing herd, nor the language of the otherworldly celibate who seeks God alone as spouse. He refuses to be Burns. He refuses to be Hopkins. He is Cairns, who chronicles lay ascesis in an Eastern-tinged English verse. Between the kontakia-like poems can still be found pentameter, sometimes even sonnets. And between the careful, oft-retraced steps toward God, Cairns still wants to meet with his reader over a coffee or a beer. But he also will invite the reader, over that drink, on a pilgrimage to Mount Athos, so one can mix with monks. This lay casualness mixed with lay ascesis is part of what put off Klug, but it is indicative of Orthodox Christianity in America, and, curiously, is part of the Orthodox poetic tradition: neither Saint Ephrem nor Saint Romanos were monks or priests. Rather, they were involved in the liturgical life of the church as readers, as deacons, as choir members.

In closing, let us turn to Ephrem's contemporary, Gregory Nazianzus, a poet who Cairns also translated in *Love's Immensity*. According to Saint Gregory, poetic endeavor, like spiritual endeavor, is primarily ascetic:

> With measured labor—first—I discipline my soul,
> For writing lines may order my unmetered mind
> And keep my greedy pen in check—instead I spend
> My sweat on metric form.[10]

Cairns takes the same ascetic approach to both poetry and spirituality. While Gregory located the toil primarily in the effort to write according to the demands of classical meter, Cairns applies his toil at the level of sentence structure, seeking to create in his readers a sense of ascetic endeavor as they become the slow pilgrim traveling the narrow road of his lines. Before the soul can drown in God, Cairns reminds us, it must hobble toward him. And anyone can hobble, he nudges us to agree, if they so choose.

---

10. Gregory Nazianzus, "Eis Ta Emmetra," ll. 33–37.

9

Conclusion
The Literary Conservationist

THE ESSAYS IN THIS book, taken together, call for something of a recentering in our conception of literary history. This recentering is twofold. First, I have suggested that the Church Fathers, especially the poetry of the Church Fathers, is a center from which we might look in our interpretation and estimation of the literature of later centuries. Second, I have suggested that such a vantage point might highlight certain poets of our recent tradition who have not always been sufficiently attended to. Thus, to treat Gregory Nazianzus and Prudentius as central literary figures of late antiquity prepares us to see the patristic influence and resonance in not only canonical poets such as Milton and Eliot but also in poets like Longfellow and Browning, who in their own day were world-famous, but today are relegated to a decidedly minor status.

Further, the explicitly theological subjects and critical outlook of the Church Fathers can help us read the poetry of our own day with a sort of robust confidence in the theological nature of literary art. To read Milton or Longfellow from the vantage point of classical antiquity is to be continually distracted and annoyed at their thoroughly Christian and incessantly biblical subjects.

Conclusion

But from a patristic viewpoint, this interest in theological subjects is perfectly natural and integrated into a larger aesthetic, cultural, and political vision. Longfellow's abolitionism, far from being a progressive quirk in an otherwise staid conservatism, proves to be an outworking of his theological anthropology and ethics, grounded in a metaphysics of human personhood and destiny which the poet drew from a long line of Christian poets, including the Spanish mystics, Dante, and, ultimately, the Church Fathers, especially Chrysostom and Lactantius.

Where, then, do we go from here? Simply put, the poetry of the patristic age must be recovered as required reading for the aspiring poet and critic. If Eliot apprenticed himself to Prudentius, if Browning apprenticed herself to Gregory, then we are not above the same apprenticeship. But the poetry of late antiquity is, at the present time, much less accessible to the average reader than the poetry of, say, Homer or Dante. This is largely due to the lack of affordable translations from major publishers. Remedying this would take not merely more editorial interest in late antique poetry, but an interest by translators in focusing on the poetry of that era. As of 2023 we are in something of a golden age of formal translations of ancient Greek poetry: new translations of Homer, Hesiod, and Sappho appear regularly by master poet-translators like A. E. Stallings, Emily Wilson, and Jim Powell. If these translators would turn their attentions to Prudentius or Proba, we might begin to more practically enable the aforementioned re-centering.[1]

We have already discussed in the introduction how educators bear much of the responsibility for shaping each generation's conception of literary history. The translators and publishers, then, can only accomplish half the work. And the true success of such a recentering will be something hardly imaginable in our current culture: it would be a widespread national and even international imagination in which the early Church provides our central

---

[1]. This is not to say that there have been no good metrical translations of early Christian poetry. Sister M. Clement Eagan's renderings of Prudentius, in *The Poems of Prudentius* from CUA Press, for instance, are considerable poetic feats in their own right and remain in print over 60 years after their first publication.

narratives, heroes, villains, ethical language, political concerns, and ultimate questions. We in America, however, live in a culture that has a difficult time prizing any age but the present. We catch glimpses of what could be when we recover, for a moment, a winsome vision of the past in our cultural imagination—as occurred during the interest in the Peloponnesian war during the popularity of the action film *300* or the American Revolution during the popularity of the Broadway musical *Hamilton*. But these are mere fads compared to what could be. We could have generations of Americans with a common vision of history derived from a robust education and an arts and entertainment scene that draws its subjects and stories, its values and vision, from this educational foundation. Instead, we have it all backward. Our measly common curriculum—gouged, twisted, and starved by both ends of the political spectrum—provides neither a history-spanning vision nor even, it seems, basic historical facts, lest the Holocaust deniers on one side or the Gulag deniers on the other complain to their school board or preferred presidential candidate. It is left up to our entertainers—writers, directors, actors—to remind us of the past. King's march to Selma, Lincoln's and Washington's presidencies, Shakespeare's affairs of the heart and stage: we learn first of these things through entertainment and afterward educate ourselves on their historical details, having glossed over or completely ignored them in our education. And when Shakespeare is reduced to a historical footnote in our education—either through political agenda, pedagogical laziness, or the former used as an excuse for the latter—how much more have we utterly abandoned Juvencus or Ephrem?

    The early Church provides, I think, a way through the polarization and wrongheadedness of our present. Even the language I have used about cultural imagination and tradition is dangerous, especially because this language is used by those who would champion a particular, historically myopic, nationalist vision of education. More conservative communities in America are tempted by a simplistic, triumphalist vision, in which American leaders, culture, and values have always been heroic, successful, and uniquely

Conclusion

correct, and all other countries and traditions have been ruinously wrong. Of course, this creates a counter-narrative in which American leaders, culture, and values are the most insidiously evil to ever desecrate the earth. But both views give the whole American experiment too much credit. From the wide vantage point of the distant past, America is one among many places and cultures in which humans have tried and often failed to live well. We are neither uniquely oppressed nor uniquely blessed, and our literary achievements, as Eliot argued, ought to be assessed among the library of the ages, held to the same standards that we would hold the classics of ancient China or medieval Norway.[2]

The early Church knew that human life and flourishing can never depend on the actions of one ruler, one state, one ethnic group. The monotheism of the patristic vision might lead some to infer that it must also be mono-lingual and mono-cultural. But if God is the ground of all being, the King of all kings, and the Lord of all lords, then a patristic vision can be robustly multi-linguistic, multi-ethnic, multi-cultural, and its estimation of literary art can avoid the narrow meanness of the jingoist and the cultural supremacist.

In closing, I would like to draw in a borrowed image: that of the conservationist and the gardener. I have often been taken with the idea that political conservatism and environmental conservationism should be more closely allied. Both share a sense that there are old and enduring things that ought to be conserved not only because they were once valuable, but because they are still valuable. The conservative desires to retain something like religious freedom for the same reason that the conservationist wants to retain something like the Grand Canyon: they each seem to be gifts from the past far outstripping the deserving of the present, and so worth fighting to preserve for the future. Both, of course, are dangerous things: religious debate in the public square can turn traumatic, as can cliffs and river-rapids when approached without due care. If literary history is a garden, then my preceding argument is that, through our ignoring of the literary foundations of

2. See Eliot, *Sacred Wood*, 49–50.

early Christianity, we have been letting the chrysanthemums wither while we water only the marigolds and roses. This is improper conservation. It is bad gardening. And in the end, is not the educator a type of gardener? I hope we teachers do not think of ourselves as mere databases from which students download facts. Neither should we fancy ourselves gurus before whom students bow or grovel. No, we are gardeners, as our mother Eve and our father Adam were. We are gardeners, as were the nuns and monks who preserved Western culture past the fall of Rome. We are gardeners who tend the flora of the past. We invite our students to come close to these old works, these ancient, living forms to which we owe so much, and breathe deep. We prune and graft curricula together. Our classrooms can be hospitable soil. We learn ourselves what keeps these works alive, and we model for our students cultivation, conservation, care. We must be gardeners, I say. We must.

Because the winter always comes around, we must. Because the soil always needs replenishing, we must. We fool ourselves to think our time especially hostile, especially depraved. The gardener takes rough weather and the changing seasons as a given. Every year the harvest is plentiful. Every year the workers are few. Be gardeners, not databases. Be gardeners, not drones. Garden with faith. Garden with hope. Garden with love.

Bibliography

Athanasius. "Letter XXXIX." In *Nicene and Post Nicene Fathers Series II, Athanasius, Selected Works and Letters*, 4:551–52. New York: Christian Literature Company, 1892.

Bartel, Timothy E. G. *Glimpses of Her Father's Glory: Deification and Divine Light in Longfellow's Evangeline*. Eugene, OR: Wipf & Stock, 2019.

———. *The Heroines of Henry Longfellow: Domestic, Defiant, Divine*. New York: Lexington, 2022.

Basil the Great. *Essays on the Study and Use of Poetry by Plutarch and St. Basil the Great*. Translated by Frederick Morgan Paddelford. New York: Holt, 1903.

———. *On Social Justice*. Translated by C. Paul Schroder. Crestwood, NY: St. Vladimir's Seminary Press, 2010.

———. *On the Human Condition*. Translated by Nonna Verna Harrison. Crestwood, NY: St. Vladimir's Seminary Press, 2005.

Browning, Elizabeth Barrett. *Essays on the Greek Christian Poets and the English Poets*. New York: Miller, 1863.

———. *The Poems of Elizabeth Barrett Browning*. New York: Warne, 1850.

Butler, Judith. "Imitation and Gender Insubordination." In *Literary Theory: An Anthology*, edited by Julie Rivkin and Michael Ryan, 955–62. Malden, MA: Wiley Blackwell, 2017.

Cairns, Scott. *Love's Immensity: Mystics on the Endless Life*. Brewster, MA: Paraclete, 2007.

———. *Slow Pilgrim: The Collected Poems*. Brewster, MA: Paraclete, 2015.

Carter, Humphrey. *The Inklings*. London: Allen & Unwin, 1978.

Channing, William E. *Slavery*. Boston: Munroe, 1835.

Cotten, Lyman. "Eliot's The Wasteland, I, 43–46." *The Explicator* 9 (1950) 10–12.

Dickens, Charles. *American Notes: For General Circulation*. London: Chapman & Hall, 1850.

Dostoevsky, Fyodor. *The Idiot*. Translated by Richard Pevear and Larissa Volokhonsky. New York: Vintage, 2003.

Douglass, Frederick. *Narrative of the Life of Frederick Douglass, an American Slave: Critical Edition*. New Haven, CT: Yale University Press, 2016.

BIBLIOGRAPHY

Duriez, Colin. *The Oxford Inklings: Lewis, Tolkien, and Their Circle.* Oxford: Lion, 2015.

Eliot, T. S. *The Complete Prose of T. S. Eliot: The Critical Edition.* Vol. 3, *Literature, Politics, Belief, 1927–1929.* Baltimore: Johns Hopkins University Press, 2015.

———. *The Letters of T. S. Eliot.* Vol. 1, *1898–1922.* New Haven, CT: Yale University Press, 2011.

———. *The Letters of T. S. Eliot.* Vol. 2, *1923–1925.* New Haven, CT: Yale University Press, 2011.

———. *Poems.* New York: Knopf, 1920.

———. *The Poems of T. S. Eliot.* Vol. 1. Baltimore: Johns Hopkins University Press, 2015.

———. *The Sacred Wood: Essays on Poetry and Criticism.* London: Methuen, 1920.

———. *Selected Essays.* New York: Farrar, Straus & Giroux, 1975.

———. *The Varieties of Metaphysical Poetry.* New York: Harvest, 1993.

———. *The Waste Land.* New York: Liveright, 1922.

———. *The Waste Land: A Facsimile and Transcript of the Original Drafts including the Annotations of Ezra Pound.* Edited by Valerie Eliot. New York: Harvest, 1971.

Eusebius. *The History of the Church.* Translated by Andrew Louth. New York: Penguin, 1989.

Gale, Robert L. *A Henry Wadsworth Longfellow Companion.* Westport, CT: Greenwood, 2003.

Gioia, Dana. *Disappearing Ink: Poetry at the End of Print Culture.* Saint Paul, MN: Graywolf, 2004.

Gregory Nazianzus. "Eis Ta Emmetra." Translated by Timothy E. G. Bartel. In *A Crown for Abba Moses: New and Selected Poems*, 77–82. Mesa, AZ: Solum Literary, 2023.

———. "The First Theological Oration." In *Nicene and Post-Nicene Fathers: Second Series: Cyril of Jerusalem and Gregory Nazianzen*, edited by Philip Schaff and Henry Wace, 7:284–88. Edinburgh: T. & T. Clark, 1894.

———. *On God and Man: The Theological Poetry of Gregory Nazianzus.* Translated by Peter L. Gilbert. Crestwood, NY: St. Vladimir's Seminary Press, 2001.

———. "Oration on the Great S. Basil." In *Nicene and Post-Nicene Fathers: Second Series: Cyril of Jerusalem and Gregory Nazianzen*, edited by Philip Schaff and Henry Wace, 7:395–422. Edinburgh: T. & T. Clark, 1894.

———. *Poemata Arcana.* Translated by D. A. Sykes. Oxford: Clarendon, 1997.

———. *Poems on Scripture.* Translated by Brian Dunkle. Crestwood, NY: St. Vladimir's Seminary Press, 2012.

———. "The Second Theological Oration." In *Nicene and Post-Nicene Fathers: Second Series: Cyril of Jerusalem and Gregory Nazianzen*, edited by Philip Schaff and Henry Wace, 7:288–301. Edinburgh: T. & T. Clark, 1894.

BIBLIOGRAPHY

Gregory of Nyssa. *The Life of Macrina*. Translated by W. K. Lowther Clarke. London: SPCK, 1916.

———. *On the Making of Man*. Translated by H. A. Wilson. In *Nicene and Post-Nicene Fathers, Second Series: Gregory of Nyssa: Dogmatic Treatises*, edited by Philip Schaff and Henry Wace, 5:387–427. Buffalo, NY: Christian Literature Publishing, 1893.

———. *On the Soul and Resurrection*. Translated by Catherine P. Routh. Crestwood, NY: St. Vladimir's Seminary Press, 1993.

Grotius, Hugo. *Christ's Passion: A Tragedie with Annotations*. Translated by George Sandys. London: Legatt, 1640.

Harris, Janet. "Longfellow's Poems on Slavery." *Colby Quarterly* 14 (1978) 84–92.

Harrison, Nonna Verna. *God's Many-Splendored Image: Theological Anthropology for Christian Formation*. Grand Rapids, MI: Baker Academic, 2010.

Hesiod. *Theogony*. Translated by Hugh Gerard Evelyn-White. Cambridge, MA: Harvard University Press, 1914.

Hooper, Walter. *C. S. Lewis: A Biography*. New York: HarperCollins, 2002.

———. *C. S. Lewis: A Companion and Guide*. New York: HarperCollins, 2006.

Huttar, Charles A. "C. S. Lewis's Appreciation of T. S. Eliot." In *T. S. Eliot and Christian Tradition*, edited by Benjamin G. Lockerd, 265–84. Madison, WI: Farleigh Dickinson University Press, 2014.

Klug, Nate. "Upside of Terror? A Review of *Compass of Affection* by Scott Cairns and *Yellowrocket* by Todd Boss." *Poetry* 193 (2009) 457–64.

Lactantius. "The Phoenix." In *Early Latin Christian Poets*, edited by Carolinne White, 28–43. London: Routledge, 2000.

Leith, John H., ed. *Creeds of the Churches*. Louisville, KY: Westminster John Knox, 1982.

Lepore, Jill. "How Longfellow Woke the Dead." *The American Scholar* 81 (2011) 2–15.

Lewis, C. S. *The Allegory of Love: A Study in Medieval Tradition*. Cambridge: Cambridge University Press, 2012.

———. *The Great Divorce*. New York: HarperCollins, 2000.

Longfellow, Henry Wadsworth. *Christus: A Mystery*. Cambridge, MA: Houghton Mifflin, 1886.

———. *The Complete Poetical Works of Henry Wadsworth Longfellow: Household Edition*. Cambridge, MA: Belknap, 1907.

———. *Final Memorials*. Boston: Ticknor, 1887.

———. *Kavanagh: A Tale*. Boston: Ticknor, Reed, & Fields, 1849.

———. *The Letters of Henry Wadsworth Longfellow*. Vol. 2. Cambridge, MA: Belknap, 1966.

———. "The Lives of Literary Men." MS Am 1340, 55, Houghton Library: Harvard University.

———. "The Soul." *The Knickerbocker: New York Monthly Magazine* 5 (January 1835) 71.

BIBLIOGRAPHY

Longfellow, Samuel. *Life of Henry Wadsworth Longfellow.* Vol. 1. Boston: Houghton, Mifflin, 1891.
McGuckin, John. *Saint Gregory of Nazianzus: An Intellectual Biography.* Crestwood, NY: St Vladimir's Seminary Press, 2001.
Milton, John. *A Common-Place Book of John Milton.* Westminster, UK: Camden Society, 1886.
———. *The Major Works.* New York: Oxford University Press, 2003.
Molinos, Miguel de. *The Spiritual Guide.* Glasgow, UK: Thomson, 1885.
Mosheim, Johann. *An Ecclesiastical History, Ancient and Modern, from the Birth of Christ, to the Beginning of the Present Century.* Translated by Archibald MacLaine. New York: Duyckinck, 1824.
Nussbaum, Martha. "Cultivating Humanity: The Narrative Imagination." In *Literary Theory: An Anthology,* edited by Julie Rivkin and Michael Ryan, 382–401. Malden, MA: Wiley Blackwell, 2017.
O'Daly, Gerard. *Days Linked by Song: Prudentius' Cathemerinon.* Oxford: Oxford University Press, 2012.
Perl, Jeffrey. "Disambivalent Quatrains." In *A Companion to T. S. Eliot,* edited by David E. Chinitz, 133–44. Oxford: Wiley Blackwell, 2009.
Poe, Edgar Allan. "Review of Henry Wadsworth Longfellow, *Poems.*" *Aristidean* (1845) 130–42.
Pope, Alexander. *The Rape of the Lock and Other Poems.* New York: Signet Classics, 2003.
Prudentius. *The Poems of Prudentius.* Vol. 2. Translated by Sister M. Clement Eagan. Washington, DC: Catholic University of America Press, 1962.
———. *Prudentius.* Vol. 1. Edited by H. J. Thomson. Cambridge, MA: Harvard University Press, 1949.
Quasten, Joannes. *Patrology.* Vol. 3, *The Golden Age of Greek Patristic Literature.* Notre Dame, IN: Christian Classics, 1983.
———. *Patrology.* Vol. 4, *The Golden Age of Latin Patristic Literature.* Edited by Angelo Di Berardino. Allen, TX: Christian Classics, 1983.
Rand, Edward Kenneth. "Prudentius and Christian Humanism." *Transactions and Proceedings of the American Philological Association* 15 (1920) 71–83.
Romanos the Melodist. "On the Nativity of Christ." Translated by Timothy E. G. Bartel. In *A Crown for Abba Moses: New and Selected Poems,* 109. Phoenix, AZ: Solum Literary Press, 2023.
Thielman, Frank. "The Place of Apocalypse in the Canon of St Gregory Nazianzen." *Tyndale Bulletin* 49 (1998) 155–57.
Thompson, Lawrance. *Young Longfellow.* New York: Octagon, 1969.
Wagenknecht, Edward. *Longfellow: A Full-Length Portrait.* New York: Longmans, Green, 1955.
White, Carolinne. *Early Latin Christian Poets.* London: Routledge, 2000.
Whittier, John Greenleaf. *Letters of John Greenleaf Whittier.* Vol. 3, *1861–1892.* Cambridge, MA: Belknap, 1975.

BIBLIOGRAPHY

Willis, Lloyd. "Feeling, Controlling, Transcending: The Negotiation of Sentiment in Longfellow, Poe, and Whitman." In *Reconsidering Longfellow*, 33–52. Madison, TN: Farleigh Dickinson University Press, 2014.

Zaleski, Carol, and Philip Zaleski. *The Fellowship: The Literary Lives of the Inklings*. New York: Farrar, Straus & Giroux, 2015.

www.ingramcontent.com/pod-product-compliance
Lightning Source LLC
Chambersburg PA
CBHW071454160426
43195CB00013B/2103